'*Lend Me Your Ears* ... ...the art of effective spea... ... ...all those interested in making words count and using verbal communication to influence people.'

Paddy Ashdown,
Leader of the Liberal Democrats, 1988–99

'This excellent book [*Lend Me Your Ears*] covers the perils of PowerPoint presentations, the power of rhetoric and how to prepare speeches when in a rush. It's clear, reassuring and useful. (Best of its kind.)'

Management Today

'Neither politicians nor business leaders can lead today without the ability to communicate effectively with audiences of all sizes or compositions. They have two choices: (1) be born with the ability, or (2) read Max Atkinson's books and learn.'

Michael Sheehan,
Former speech coach to Bill Clinton, and President, Sheehan Associates, Washington, D.C.

'No one surpasses Atkinson in the rigor and clarity with which he spells out how to move audiences to applause, get quoted in the media and become known as the most brilliant presence on any podium.'

Clark Judge,
Managing Director, White House Writers Group

Speech-making and Presentation Made Easy

Seven essential steps to success

Max Atkinson

LONDON

For Peter Semper, O.P.

1 3 5 7 9 10 8 6 4 2

Published in 2008 by Vermilion, an imprint
of Ebury Publishing

Ebury Publishing is a Random House Group company

Copyright © Max Atkinson 2008

Max Atkinson has asserted his right to be identified as the
author of this Work in accordance with the Copyright, Designs
and Patents Act 1988

The Random House Group Limited Reg. No. 954009

Addresses for companies within the Random House Group can
be found at www.rbooks.co.uk

A CIP catalogue record for this book is available from the
British Library

Mixed Sources
Product group from well-managed
forests and other controlled sources
www.fsc.org Cert no. TF-COC-2139
© 1996 Forest Stewardship Council

The Random House Group Limited supports The Forest
Stewardship Council (FSC), the leading international forest
certification organisation. All our titles that are printed on
Greenpeace approved FSC certified paper carry the FSC logo.
Our paper procurement policy can be found at
www.rbooks.co.uk/environment

Printed and bound in Great Britain by
CPI Cox & Wyman, Reading, RG1 8EX

ISBN 9780091922061

Copies are available at special rates for bulk orders.
Contact the sales development team on 020 7840 8487
for more information.

To buy books by your favourite authors and register for offers,
visit www.rbooks.co.uk

The information in this book is general in nature and not intended to constitute nor be
relied on for professional advice. The author and publishers disclaim, as far as the law
allows, any liability arising directly or indirectly from the use or misuse of the
information contained in this book.

Contents

Acknowledgements

My biggest debt of thanks is to Peter Semper, whose idea it was that I should write this book, and whose enthusiasm for the project was manifested in the huge amounts of time he spent in helping me to do it.

I am also grateful to Julia Kellaway at Vermilion, for her considerable editorial efforts in showing me how to set about reworking the original manuscript.

Finally, I must thank my wife, Joey, for taking the time to read yet another draft book and for being such an astute critic of anything that smacks of verbosity, incomprehensibility or management gobbledygook. However, any faults that remain are entirely my own responsibility.

Max Atkinson
Westbury-sub-Mendip, Somerset
www.speaking.co.uk

Introduction

Speaking to Listeners

There can be few people who have never had to sit through wedding speeches that conveyed more bad taste than good cheer, or eulogies at funerals that demonstrated little more than the speaker's total ignorance about the life and character of the deceased. Countless times a day, audiences the world over are being subjected to speeches, presentations, sermons, briefings and lectures that are inaudible, incomprehensible or uninspiring. And, when it comes to inflicting maximum pain on listeners, there are few styles of speaking more stultifying than the modern slide-driven presentation.

Most of us find it easy enough to discuss aspects of our life or work with one or two colleagues or friends, or even with complete strangers. But it's a very different story when it comes to standing up and talking about the same subjects to an audience.

Confident communicators suddenly find themselves crippled by nerves; the normally articulate sound muddled and confused; and enthusiasts for their subjects come across as dull, boring and monotonous.

This difference in our level of confidence and effectiveness, depending on whether we're speaking in a conversation or to an audience, is so great and debilitating for so many people that it demands an explanation. This book provides an answer by showing how to use the 'language of public speaking'. This is easier to learn and much less complicated than a foreign language, and is an essential first step towards understanding and mastering the techniques of effective speech-making.

The problem with public speaking, in all its various manifestations, lies in a profound and widespread misunderstanding of how spoken communication works. Somewhere along the line, speakers seem to have stopped thinking about the needs and preferences of their audiences. 'The customer is always right' may have become a standard motto in the world of business, but the idea that 'the audience is always right' has yet to make much of an impression on the world of presentation, even though, for the duration of the presentation at least, the audience is the speaker's only customer.

If the battle against boredom is to be won, a

crucial first step is to be clear about the problems faced by audiences. Only then does it become possible to come up with practical solutions that will give listeners a more rewarding and inspiring experience. Once you understand the techniques that impress audiences, you are well on the way to mastering them. You'll discover how to liberate yourself from the all-too-familiar feelings of nervousness and fear that come with the prospect of having to make a speech or presentation. And once you start putting them into practice, you'll realise that effective speech-making and presentation doesn't have to be the monopoly of a gifted few, but is the product of a set of simple techniques that anyone can learn to use.

Step 1

Keeping Audiences Engaged

Speaking in public is different from just about any other form of communication we ever get involved in. It requires skills other than those that serve us perfectly well during the rest of our talking lives. In particular, it differs from two much more familiar forms of communication: the language of conversation, and the language of the written word. Understanding what these differences are is an essential first step towards mastering the techniques of effective speech-making and presentation.

Why Audiences Fall Asleep

Speeches and Presentations are Long
In conversation, we take it in turns to speak. We have to pay attention only to short bursts of talk averaging seven or eight seconds. Members of an audience, on the other hand, are faced with having

to listen to one person speaking continuously for 10, 20 or 30 minutes – or longer!

Audiences are Passive

As conversationalists, we pay very close attention because we know that we'll have to respond as soon as the other person stops speaking. This puts continual pressure on us to listen. However, if you know you're not going to have to say anything for the next half hour or more, your incentive to pay attention is massively reduced, sometimes so much so that you find it difficult to stay awake.

Audiences are Confused

In conversation we can solve any problems we have in understanding what someone just said by asking them for clarification. When sitting in an audience, though, we feel inhibited about doing this, and often stop making any further effort to follow what the speaker is talking about. This means that your main challenge as a speaker is to make sure you present your subject matter in a way that is simple enough for anyone in the audience to understand (*see Step 2, page 35*).

Conversing With A Crowd

Winning and holding an audience's attention can never be taken for granted. It's a far greater challenge than many speakers realise, and is a battle you have to fight relentlessly for the entire duration of any speech or presentation. This is why it's so important to be clear about the nature of the beast we're up against, and about the weapons available to keep audiences awake and defeat the ever-present threat of boredom.

It's sometimes possible to win minor victories by interacting more directly with the audience because our level of attentiveness will increase if we have a chance to respond to what a speaker says. When audiences become involved in a speech or presentation, it tends to generate a good deal more liveliness and interest. Two important responses that can help keep an audience attentive are laughter and participation.

Laughter

Audiences obviously enjoy laughing: it's not only proof that they enjoyed or approved of something you said, but it's also a powerful spur to continued attentiveness. Once we have laughed for a first time, we start looking out for more fun and a chance to laugh again. Even if none comes immediately, you can be sure that everyone will be listening closely to whatever you say next. Being on the receiving end of such a positive response will also make you feel better and give your confidence a boost.

If audiences laugh at a humorous anecdote that illustrates a key point, it makes it more likely that they'll remember it in the longer term. A successful lawyer once said that the one situation where he could be 90 per cent certain that a jury would find in his client's favour was if, during his final address to them, he had made them laugh.

Audience Participation

Another way to reproduce the kind of pressure to pay attention that's involved when taking it in turns to speak in a conversation is by getting the audience to do or say something. This might simply involve asking for a show of hands, inviting suggestions or embarking on a question-and-answer session. As every teacher knows, getting pupils to answer questions can be a very effective way of keeping them on their toes. Once we realise that the speaker is no longer treating us as passive listeners but might fire a question at us at any moment, we know that it's time to start listening closely enough to be able to say something if and when we are spoken to.

Audience Interruptions

Another type of audience participation comes when speakers invite members of an audience to intervene with questions whenever they feel like it. This is a risky strategy that's best avoided, unless your main objective is to stimulate a discussion on issues raised by the audience. The problem with unsolicited contributions is that they can easily knock you off course, and may even take up so much time that you have to rush through the later sections of the presentation, or perhaps even miss them out altogether.

Interruptive questions often raise issues that you are planning to deal with later on. So a much safer option is to make it clear at the outset that there will be plenty of time for questions at the end.

Eye Contact And Attentiveness

In the battle for attention and understanding, one conversational resource that retains much of its power when addressing audiences is eye contact between speaker and hearers.

Use Gaze to Increase Attention

The more you look at the audience, the more likely they are at least to try and look as though they are paying attention. If you focus on one individual in the audience for more than a second or two, they're likely to nod or smile in response. It's as if they feel obliged to confirm that they're awake, listening and on track with what you're saying. Remember that audiences are not made up of people all wired up together but of separate, unique individuals, not much different from yourself.

Use Gaze to Check Audience Reactions

Nods, smiles and other non-verbal responses, such as writing notes, usually mean that things are going well. On the other side of the coin, we ignore yawns, head scratching and other signs of puzzlement or boredom at our peril. The most usual problem is that the audience is losing the thread, in which case it's a good idea to try a different way of clarifying the point that seems to be causing the trouble.

Use Gaze to Engage the Audience

Audiences appreciate eye contact because it makes them feel that you are talking directly to them. So if you don't look at them, or if your eyes spend most of their time glued to a script or notes, it gives the impression that ploughing through the text is more important than communicating and relating to the people in front of you.

Don't Gaze at the Screen

When they see themselves on video, many speakers are amazed to discover just how long they spent looking back at their slides. 'Touch, turn and talk' provides a useful reminder that glances at the screen should be short and quickly followed by a resumption of more extended eye contact with the audience.

Don't Engage in Phoney Eye Contact

'Phoney' or simulated eye contact is something that most of us have experienced when sitting in an audience. This is when the speaker's eyes spend most of their time scanning along the line where the ceiling joins the wall at the back of the room, along the top of the tables in front of the audience or even along the feet of those on the front row. This is not a good idea as it cuts out the audience and suggests that you're afraid of what you might see if you actually look at them. It's also likely to raise questions in their minds about your confidence and command over the subject matter.

Avoid Skewed Eye Contact

This is when a speaker spends much more time looking at one part of the audience than another, which has the effect of making anyone sitting on the 'wrong' side of the room feel left out.

Some speakers concentrate most of their attention on those whom they consider to be the most important people in the room. The danger here is that it will look as though you are discriminating between senior and junior members, or trying to ingratiate yourself with the powers that be.

Don't be Afraid to Look Down and Up

Speakers often worry about losing eye contact when referring to notes or a script. Although looking down more or less continuously has a negative impact on the audience, regular glances up and down are not really a problem and are often hardly even noticed by the audience. After all, some politicians can deliver inspiring speeches when reading a script on a lectern. The point is that eye contact doesn't have to be continuous, and people may even find it uncomfortable if they feel that you are staring at them all the time.

Differences Between Public Speaking And Conversation

When you're in front of an audience, speaking in the same way as you do in a conversation is not much help in solving problems of attentiveness and understanding. Here we will look at some important reasons why you need to modify your usual style of speaking when making a speech or presentation.

Conversational Pauses

We usually try to avoid periods of silence when speaking conversationally. Often we do this by punctuating much of what we say with 'ums' and 'ers'. Though hardly noticeable in a conversation, this can be very irritating to an audience. It also makes you sound hesitant, uncertain of your material and badly prepared.

In conversation, 'ums' and 'ers' are also commonly used at the start of a new speaker's turn. This is no doubt why some public speakers make a habit of starting almost every new sentence with an 'um' or an 'er'. It's something they are completely unaware of until they hear themselves on tape – when they are typically appalled by the negative impression they must have been giving.

We also tend to 'um' or 'er' in conversations when we are suddenly at a loss for the word or name we need to be able to carry on. If we simply pause while searching for the right word, the chances are that someone else will seize upon the silence and start speaking, preventing us from finishing the point we were trying to make. In this context, we use 'ums' and 'ers' to let everyone know that we still have more to say and that they should wait until we've finished.

Periods of silence in conversations often cause trouble or embarrassment. In fact, pauses lasting longer than half a second are extremely rare because we collaborate with each other to ensure that silences are few and far between. The trouble is that we're so used to doing this that our natural instinct is to carry on doing it when speaking to an audience.

If a speaker doesn't pause, and fills every possible silence with an 'um' or an 'er', this is guaranteed to have a negative impact on audiences. However, doing the opposite of what we do in conversation has positive advantages for both audience and speaker.

Pausing for a Purpose

Pausing and pace

Punctuating talk with much more frequent and longer silences than is normal in conversation helps audiences by breaking up the flow of ideas into short, digestible units. If you don't do this, they'll have the problem of trying to take in too much information too quickly, and may even become so overwhelmed that they stop making any further effort to follow what you're saying.

Pauses also have a number of advantages for speakers, such as helping to control their breathing. By pausing regularly and speaking more slowly than in conversation, you can reduce the pace to some-where between 120 and 130 words per minute, which is the average speed for an effective speech or presentation. As for how long and how often you should pause, there are no hard and fast rules. Some professional speechwriters believe that an average of one pause every seven words is about right. Pauses in a speech can be much longer than feels comfortable in a conversation, where half a second or more can seem interminable. However, the key to effective delivery lies in variation, both in the number of words between pauses as well as the overall pace at which different segments are delivered.

Pausing for effect

Pausing in different places can change the dramatic impact of sentences. Here, for example, is the text of the final part of Churchill's radio address to the nation after the fall of France in 1940, during which he paused six times (at the end of each line):

Let us therefore brace ourselves to our duty,
and so bear ourselves
that, if the British Empire and its Commonwealth
lasts for a thousand years,
men will still say
'This
was their finest hour.'

Listen closely to effective speakers in action, paying particular attention to where the pauses occur. Another exercise is to take the text of a speech or a newspaper article and read it aloud several times, pausing at different places. See how the meaning and emphasis change.

Pausing to plan what to say next

Even a moment's silence is long enough to give you time to glance at your notes, plan what to say next or make a slight change in direction. You might, for example, have seen signs of puzzlement or boredom from the audience, in which case you may decide to add some previously unplanned words of clarification, an illustrative example or perhaps a summary of the argument so far.

Intonation and Stress

A commonly heard complaint from audiences is that a speaker just droned on and on. The word 'drone', of course, refers to a continuous and unchanging stream of sound, and highlights the fact that speaking in a monotone is widely regarded as a bad thing. We therefore need to be clear about how variation in tone plays a positive part in the communication process. The most important thing to remember is that intonation and stress work in a similar way to pauses and provide another way of conveying different meanings and moods.

Stress

As a general guide, there will be at least one word in every sentence that needs extra stress. This is why, when using a script, it's a good idea to go through it and underline or highlight words that you plan to say with extra emphasis.

Upwards and downwards variations in tone can also make a big difference to how we interpret what we hear. Depending on how you say 'he spoke for well over an hour', you can make it sound like a statement of fact, a compliment or a complaint.

Mood

Intonation is at the heart of the way we communicate different moods and emotions like passion, conviction and enthusiasm, and plays a crucial role in holding the interest and attention of an audience.

This was clearly illustrated when a multinational corporation was launching some new products. A videotape of a short statement by the marketing director was played on a large screen to the audience. He concluded with the words, 'I hope you're all as excited by these new products as I am' – only to be greeted by loud, raucous laughter from the audience. This was because his flat intonation made him sound bored, uninterested and unenthusiastic while using words that were intended to communicate exactly the opposite.

Of all the emotions that can be conveyed through intonation, enthusiasm must surely be the most important. When people think back to their school days, the teachers they are most likely to remember with affection are the ones who were the most passionate and enthusiastic about the subjects they were teaching.

Exaggeration for Effect

Many speakers are surprised to discover that they are coming across to the audience as far more monotonous and boring than they sounded to themselves while delivering the presentation. This is more or less inevitable if you make no effort to speak any differently from the way you speak in conversation, in which slight shifts and nuances are easy for listeners to hear over a short distance. But over the much longer distance between you and your audience, such variations flatten out and sound monotonous.

The answer to this is to exaggerate your normal conversational patterns of intonation and stress. The sound will still flatten out across a distance, but the greater variations will come across as quite natural by the time they reach the ears of the audience.

Learning to do this successfully is, of course, easier said than done. Most people will initially find it rather embarrassing, and worry that they will sound stupid if they 'ham it up' too much. Most of us are not born actors, but this is not quite the same thing as acting, which requires you to come across as someone different from your normal self. When making a speech, it is only our own characteristic patterns of intonation that should be exaggerated. This may make us sound a little larger than life inside our own heads, but will come across as normal to people listening from some distance away.

As a rough guide, the bigger the audience and the bigger the room in which you are speaking, the more you'll need to exaggerate your intonation and stress. At the other end of the scale, if you're presenting to a group of fewer than about seven people, you can get away with speaking in your normal conversational tone.

Differences Between Public Speaking And Writing

There are some important differences between the way we write and the way we speak. This means that you can't rely on the written word to see you through a speech or presentation. The most common problems involve verbal and information overload.

Verbal Overload

Hyper-correct Grammar

One of the most obvious symptoms of verbal overload is the production of grammatically faultless sentences of a kind that are hardly ever heard in everyday speech. For example, try reading aloud the following statements from former British Prime Minister John Major, and you'll find just how stilted they sound:

> 'I used to call in at wayside hostelries with whomsoever I happened to be.'
> 'On the morrow of my defeat, I bade farewell to Downing Street...'

Words: The Simpler the Better

Using words that are hardly ever heard in everyday speech will also make it more difficult for an audience to understand the point you're trying to get across. The two columns in the example opposite contain sentences that convey the same message, but the lines on the left and right use different words. Just how much difference the alternative wording makes to the degree of formality and comprehensibility becomes apparent as soon as you try reading the two versions aloud.

Formal/written	**Informal/spoken**
We shall endeavour to commence	We shall try to begin
the enhancement programme forthwith	the repairs immediately
in order to ensure that	so that
there is sufficient time	there's enough time
to facilitate the dissemination of	to send
the relevant contractual documentation	the contracts
to purchasers ahead of the renovations	to buyers before the work
being brought to completion.	is finished.

Jargon and acronyms

Our language gives us a huge choice of words. Wherever possible, it is always worth making an effort to use simple words that are in common spoken usage. This includes avoiding any specialised, technical or analytical terms that may be second nature to you, but are unfamiliar to the audience, and to make sure that you clarify the meaning of any technical terms.

Shortened forms

Using shortened forms like 'I'll', 'you'd', 'wasn't', and so on, when addressing an audience, is likely to sound more natural and less formal than the full forms used when writing.

Street-cred, localisms and slang

Another set of words that we use frequently in everyday speech, but tend to avoid when writing, comes under the heading of street-cred, localisms and slang. When speaking to an audience, it's as well to approach the use of such language with caution. If you're reporting what someone else actually said, then there's usually no problem in including slang in a verbatim quotation. But beware of relying so heavily on colloquialisms and slang that you come across as offensive, patronising or just trying to be hip.

Sentences: The Shorter the Better

Longer sentences usually include more than one key point or idea. As a result, audiences may find too much information coming at them too quickly for them to be able to take it all in before the speaker goes on to the next sentence.

Repetition

When writing for readers, there is a powerful convention against repeating words and phrases that were used in a previous or earlier sentence. But when it comes to public speaking, this rule is turned on its head, and various forms of repetition can be very effective.

Repetition to connect sentences

When you want to group together a series of messages it is often a good idea to repeat the first few words of each one. Each of the six dreams in Martin Luther King's famous speech in Washington, DC in 1963 was made up of at least a full sentence. If he had not repeated 'I have a dream' at the start of each one, it would have been much less clear to the audience that each successive point was a component of the same overall dream:

> *I have a dream* that one day this nation will rise up and live out the true meaning of its creed. We hold these truths to be self-evident: that all men are created equal.
>
> *I have a dream* that one day on the red hills of Georgia the sons of former slaves and the sons of former slave owners will be able to sit down together at a table of brotherhood.
>
> *I have a dream* that one day even the state of Mississippi, a desert state, sweltering with the heat of injustice and oppression, will be transformed into an oasis of freedom and justice...
>
> Martin Luther King

This form of repetition can be thought of as the spoken equivalent of bullet points on a page, implicitly reminding the audience that a list of similar items is in the process of being delivered.

Repetition to increase impact
Repetition can greatly increase the impact of the message you want to get across. For example, if Winston Churchill had been writing with the repetition avoidance rule in mind, a famous excerpt from one of his wartime speeches would have looked like this:

> We shall fight on the seas and oceans, in the air, on the beaches, on the landing grounds, in the fields, streets and hills.

Read it aloud, and then compare it with the actual version, in which he repeated the words 'we shall fight' six times, the effect of which is to shift the emphasis from a list of places where fighting will take place to an unequivocal determination to *fight*.

> We shall fight on the seas and oceans,
> we shall fight... in the air...
> we shall fight on the beaches,
> we shall fight on the landing grounds,
> we shall fight in the fields and in the streets,
> we shall fight in the hills;
> we shall never surrender.
>
> **Winston Churchill**

Repetitive bogey words to avoid

Not all forms of repetition are helpful to an audience, however. Something that can easily become a distraction is the excessive repetition of a particular word or phrase. The most common bogey words of this kind are 'actually', 'basically' and 'you know'. Some speakers repeat one or other of these with such regularity that it can become as irritating to an audience as repetitive 'erring' and 'umming'.

Information Overload

Effective speaking is not just a matter of keeping the language as simple as possible; it also depends on simplifying the content. The biggest single problem with today's speeches and presentations is that far too many speakers spend far too much time trying to get far more detailed information across than it's possible to convey within the limitations of the spoken word. Audiences are subjected to massive and painful information overload that serves little or no useful purpose. At best, they will retain no more than a fraction of what was said; at worst they will give up making the effort to pay attention altogether, fall asleep and end up no wiser than they were at the start.

Our Limited Capacity to Absorb Spoken Information

The tendency of speakers to pack in as much as possible seems to reflect a widespread misunderstanding of how the spoken and written word compare when it comes to conveying large volumes of detailed information. Writing and the revolution in information technology have provided methods for storing and transmitting knowledge at levels of detail far in excess of anything that could ever be achieved solely on the basis of the spoken word.

For example, a single page of a broadsheet newspaper contains more words than a 20-minute news programme on radio or television. And it's fairly obvious that if there is a lot to say about a particular subject, there's nothing to stop us writing hundreds of pages about it. However, at a speaking rate of about 120 words per minute, it is equally obvious that half an hour will restrict us to no more than 4,000 words. Speakers then face the challenge of having to select, simplify, edit, summarise and shorten the mass of material that is potentially eligible for inclusion (*see Step 2*).

Barriers to Simplification

Slides

Unfortunately, the development of computerised slides has made it possible to project huge amounts of detail on to a screen. This has created the illusion that there is no problem in transmitting large volumes of complex and detailed information directly from a screen to the brains of the audience. And if you can put as much detail as you like up on a slide, why bother to simplify?

Fear of sounding ignorant

Some speakers resist simplification because they're afraid the audience might get a negative impression if they fail to demonstrate anything less than the full extent of their knowledge of a subject. But if you use details sparingly to develop your argument, you stand a better chance of coming across as confident and authoritative, and are much less likely to leave your audience in a battered state of bewildered incomprehension. In short, your chances of success are much greater if you simplify your subject matter beyond the point at which you, as a specialist, feel comfortable.

Introducing detailed documents

Simplification is perhaps at its most difficult when the aim of a presentation is to introduce detailed written documents like reports and proposals. A common mistake here is to try to cover as much as possible of what is already included in the accompanying written material. If people in the audience have read the report or proposal beforehand, they are likely to be much less impressed by an earnest attempt to go over all the same ground than by a lively summary of the key points. Those who haven't yet read the document are also likely to view a lively summary more positively, and to be interested enough to want to read the detailed version for themselves.

As speakers, our job is to summarise and give life to the main points. Otherwise, we serve little useful purpose as far as the audience is concerned. The job of the written document is to give them as much detail and complexity as the subject deserves, and any attempt by a speaker to reproduce it in its entirety is doomed to failure.

Step 1 Summary
Keeping Audiences Engaged

1. Audiences have serious problems in remaining attentive because:
   - speeches and presentations are too long
   - the audience has a passive role

2. Audiences are more likely to pay attention when:
   - they have a chance to join in
   - the speaker makes them laugh
   - the speaker keeps good eye contact with them

3. Make the most of eye contact:
   - Look at the audience.
   - Spend as little time as possible looking back at the screen, blackboard or flipchart – *touch, turn and talk.*
   - Look people in the eye – looking above or below their heads will not do.
   - Make sure you include everyone.
   - Don't worry about glancing down at notes – but keep it brief.

4. **Speaking to an audience is different from speaking in a conversation:**
   - Reduce 'ums' and 'ers' to a minimum.
   - Pause for longer and more frequently than when you're speaking in a conversation.
   - Vary your intonation, stress and emphasis to convey different meanings and moods.
   - Exaggerate your everyday conversational intonation.

5. **Speaking is different from writing:**
   - Don't try to speak in a 'hyper-correct' way.
   - Use simple words.
   - Keep your sentences as short and simple as possible.
   - Keep jargon and acronyms to an absolute minimum.
   - Don't use the full forms of words that are usually shortened in conversation.
   - Avoid slang and/or attempts to sound hip.
   - Use repetition to increase the impact.
   - Avoid repeating words like 'actually', 'basically' and 'you know' that serve little or no purpose.
   - Don't try to get too much information across.
   - Don't put large amounts of information on a slide.

- Simplify your content beyond the point at which you feel comfortable.
- When introducing written reports and proposals, make your summary so interesting that the audience will want to go away and read it for themselves.

Step 2

Preparing, Planning and Structure

The overall structure of a speech or presentation plays a crucial part in its resulting impact on an audience. Without shape and planning, it is doomed to failure. A coherent structure will not only help the audience to follow your thoughts and argument, but will also make it easier for you to stay on track and say the things you want to say. This applies to every kind of speech or presentation, whether in a political, business, social or any other setting.

It is not enough simply to get some slides together with a view to ad-libbing your way through a list of bullet points, as is standard practice in many management and business presentations (*see Step 3 for more detail on the pitfalls of this*). Sometimes, people who use the 'slides-first' method of preparation worry that any alternative approach will take far more time and effort than they have available.

The approach taken in this book has been developed in direct response to such fears. It provides a systematic method of preparation to enable you to plan well-structured presentations that will achieve maximum impact in a minimum amount of time.

My method involves a seven-stage process. It not only helps with the creation of a tight, easy-to-follow sequence, but also prepares you for the moment when you deliver it:

1   Analysing the audience
2   Brainstorming the topic
3   Creating the structure
4   Saying it creatively
5   Creating the visual aids
6   Rehearsal
7   Preparing for question time (optional)

Analysing The Audience

Although preparing a speech obviously involves planning what to say, it's useful to think of the process as one of planning listening time for your audience. In particular, you need to take into account who is going to be in the audience, how many are going to be present and what kind of message is likely to be appropriate.

Who's in the Audience?

It is important to take the composition and interests of your audience into account right from the start. You need to have some idea of how much they are likely to know about the subject matter, and how to deal with it if the audience is made up of a mixture of specialists and non-specialists. The safest solution is to pitch it towards the non-specialists, as the specialists in the audience will, like you, be aware of the different levels of expertise among those present. So they're likely to understand and appreciate your concern for making things intelligible for everyone.

How Big is the Audience?

The bigger the audience, the greater the diversity of backgrounds and levels of knowledge will tend to be. This means that the anticipated size of an audience will also have a bearing on the level at which the subject matter should be pitched: in general, the larger the audience, the simpler the content should be.

The numbers present will also affect other issues, such as what kinds of visual aids will be appropriate, and whether or not to rely on notes or to use a full script. With small audiences, it is rarely appropriate to read a speech verbatim from a text. But many speakers feel safer speaking from a text when addressing 50 or 100 people. When timing is of critical importance, a fully scripted speech also has the advantage of making it more likely that the presentation will end on time.

What Message for this Audience?

Participants on training programmes often complain about having to sit through presentations that lack focus. The point of the presentation is often unclear, and the presentation is simply part of the way things have always been done. To avoid such uncertainty, a final and crucial step in analysing the audience is to decide on the core message to be conveyed.

First, what is the purpose of your talk? And second, what is the main message you want to get across? For example, you may want to show that management is caring, concerned and responsible, while delivering a difficult message about staff discipline. Or you may want to show that you're a forward-thinking, confident account manager, while talking about the year-end sales figures to a particular group of customers.

Given the problems of audience attentiveness and understanding, the best we can probably ever hope for is that people will go away with a grasp of the main theme or gist of what we were talking about. This is why it's so important to be absolutely clear right from the start about what, if nothing else, you want this particular audience to take away with them at the end. This then makes it possible to set about preparing and structuring in a way that will make it more likely that you succeed in getting that central theme across.

Brainstorming The Topic

The next step in preparation is to think about the topics that might be relevant to getting your key message across to the target audience. This begins with a brainstorming exercise which involves making a list of all the topics that might be included in the presentation. Once you have done this, there's a good chance that there will be far too much material, or that some of it may not be suitable for your target audience. So, in the interests of simplification and tailoring the material to your listeners, you can often start deleting some of the items straight away. One of the main problems for audiences is having to put up with speakers trying to get far too much information across in the time available. So you have to be prepared to cut your material to an extent that you may find quite painful.

Sectionalising

Brainstormed lists will typically consist of many more than the three or four sections that would make a suitable structure. The next step, then, is to organise the various items under a smaller number of headings. Go through the list with an eye to which items fit together, and which ones would be better placed in some other section. At the end of this stage, you should be left with a small number of main headings, with related topics listed under each one.

Sequencing

The order in which you write items down on a brainstormed list is likely to influence the way you order the different sections. But this won't necessarily be the best sequence for making sure the key theme gets across to the audience. You therefore need to give careful thought to the order in which you are going to present each of the sections. In general, your aim should be to organise the various parts into a coherent argument that you can develop in logical steps during the presentation. And it is particularly effective if the whole thing can be made to sound like a story with a clear message at the end of it.

Creating The Structure

Audiences can make better sense of a presentation if they are clear from the start about what it is going to cover, and the order in which the different items will be dealt with. Having a sense of what to expect gives them a set of milestones that enables them to track where the talk has got to, and – importantly – to anticipate when it is likely to finish. Without such guidelines, there is the awful prospect that it might go on for ever.

Divide your presentation into a five-part structure, in which the introductory and concluding sections are divided into two:

Pre-introduction
Introduction
Main body
Summary
Conclusion

The Pre-introduction

If it's important for audiences to have a sense of what's to come, it's obviously crucial that they should be fully attentive at the point when you introduce your subject matter. Right at the start, however, you can't rely on audiences to be completely focused on what you are saying. They may still be rattling coffee cups, or chatting between themselves at the point when you start. In any event, it usually takes a few moments for them to adapt to a new speaker, so the danger of launching straight into the introduction is that not everyone will have settled down enough to take it in. And, if they miss crucial information about the structure of what's to come, they may find the talk more difficult to follow later on.

An effective pre-introduction therefore involves saying something that has no other purpose than to catch the attention of the audience and set the mood for what follows. Then, by the time you get to the introduction proper, there is a much greater chance of the audience paying full attention to it than if you had launched straight in with it during your first few words. Here are a couple of examples of good openers:

> In 2006, IDT launched around 500 new products. By 2010, this number will have increased to a staggering 1,000 new products during the year.

> I'd like to start by posing a question: is there any point in being good at something if people don't know you're good at it?

A suitable quotation, references to current affairs, something said by an earlier speaker or an anecdote can all be pressed into service to get the interest and attention of the audience. If an opening humorous remark prompts laughter, you can be sure that the audience will be listening closely to whatever you say next.

The Introduction

Once you have successfully engaged the audience with a pre-introduction, you can safely proceed to outlining the sequence of topics to be covered. And the key words here are 'sequence' and 'outline'. The idea of sequence is important because it refers to the order in which topics are dealt with and developed over a period of time. And the idea of an outline is important because it gives the audience a broad grasp of what topics to expect. It's no use putting up a slide and announcing, as I have seen speakers do, that the presentation will deal with the list of 10 or 15 topics displayed on the screen. Audiences will simply recoil at the prospect of the massive overload of information about to be inflicted on them, and are likely to switch off even before the talk has got properly under way.

For the audience to be able to grasp an overall sense of structure, you have to outline it as simply as possible and describe it clearly. There are no rules about how many sections there should be, but experience suggests that more than three or four will start to put a strain on the audience's ability to retain the overview for the duration of the talk.

The Main Body

You will already have put the topics into sections, and the sections into a sequence, during the brainstorming phase. Most of the time spent on preparation will be devoted to getting the main body together. It's useful to bear in mind that the various sections themselves, especially the longer and more important ones, can benefit from having beginnings, middles and endings.

Given that audiences cannot always be relied on to remember the overall structure for the entire duration of a presentation, they will welcome occasional reminders of 'where we've got so far', and the ground still to be covered. The use of signposts that point backwards to where we have been, and forwards to where we are going, not only helps the audience to keep on track but also reminds the speaker to stick to the structure announced at the start.

The Summary and Conclusion

Just as it's important for a presentation to get off to a good start, the way it ends can also have a critical impact on the audience. The trouble is that speakers often find it difficult to draw things to a close. In some situations, as with political or after-dinner speeches, there's a good chance that the silence at the end will be immediately filled by applause. But on most other occasions, you know that as soon as you stop speaking, you'll be confronted by an uncomfortable and seemingly endless silence. However tempting it may be to try and keep that awful moment at bay by adding just a few more words (and a few more after that), the fact has to be faced that sooner or later you will have to stop speaking.

One step towards overcoming this problem is simply to be aware of it. Another is to have a clear strategy for bringing the talk to a decisive close. This is why it's useful to treat the end of a presentation as consisting of two distinct tasks. The first is the traditional 'tell them what you told them' or, in other words, a brief summary of the main point(s). The second is to draw out from that a concluding statement that encapsulates the key message that you had decided on much earlier when analysing the audience. Given that this is the last thing the audience will hear, every attempt should be made to package it in as punchy and memorable a way as possible.

Returning to Base

One way of embarking on a closing sequence that can be very effective is to refer back to something you said during the introduction or pre-introduction. Doing this is a way of letting the audience know that the end is near in a more subtle way than with lines that explicitly refer to structural elements, such as 'in summary...' or 'to summarise...'. At the same time, the link back to the opening theme or idea makes it appear that the presentation had an impressively rounded structure and was well planned right from the start.

Saying It Creatively

None of the above stages needs to take more than a few minutes. They will, however, already have taken you a long way towards solving the problem of structure. You have decided what to say, the main headings under which to say it, and the sequence in which it will be presented. But there is another very important step for anyone who wants to have a more positive impact on the audience than presenters who use slides as prompts. This involves going beyond deciding what to say to work out how to say it in as effective a way as possible. It means looking for interesting ways to get the contents of each section across (and making as much use as you can of the toolkit of techniques described in Step 4).

Notes or Script?

Fully scripted presentations are usually more appropriate if the audience is going to be very large, or where timing is absolutely critical. Given that most speeches and presentations are to fairly small audiences, notes will usually be the most suitable aide-mémoire for the speaker. Some people, however, find it useful to write the whole thing out first, and then reduce it to shorthand headings for use when actually making the presentation. Others worry that, if they rely on notes, they won't be able to make much use of carefully phrased rhetorical lines, imagery or anecdotes.

The solution is to combine shorthand headings with fully scripted lines where they are needed. Luckily, however, people find that they don't have to do as much scripting as they expect when first setting out to incorporate the techniques described in Step 4. For example, in the case of anecdotes, metaphors and other forms of imagery, it isn't always necessary to write the whole thing out. A single written word or phrase is all you need to trigger the story or the image.

Cards or Paper?

Paper is fine if there's going to be a lectern, or if you are sitting at a table and can glance down at the sheets laid out in front of you. But when there's no such support, sheets of paper tend to flap about, which risks distracting both audience and speaker. This is where the extra stiffness of cards comes into its own. For speakers who worry about what to do with their hands, having to hold on to cards more or less solves the problem. As for what size of card to use, 10 by 15 centimetres seems to work best. And, obvious though it may seem, clear numbering of the pages or cards is a crucial defence against disasters such as dropping them on the floor.

Turning Pages

When reading from loose sheets of paper, we naturally turn each page right over so that it ends up facing downwards. The only useful purpose this serves is to make sure that the pages of the document end up in the same order as they were at the start. However, as we never have to repeat a speech or presentation as soon as it is finished, it doesn't really matter if they end up in the reverse order, as happens when each page is moved sideways onto a growing pile rather than turned over. Doing this draws less attention to the fact that you're turning a page, and removes another potential source of distraction – which can become quite serious if a microphone picks up the noise of rustling paper and amplifies it around the conference hall. It can also be unnecessarily distracting if you make a habit of dropping each card to the table as you finish with it. This is also likely to encourage members of the audience to start monitoring the ever-diminishing number of cards in your hand.

Writing Speeches

If you plan to write out the full text of a speech, it's extremely important to take into account the differences between the written and spoken word, and especially to make sure that you keep the sentences short.

An easy way to do this is to stop arranging sentences in paragraphs, and start each new sentence on a new line like this.

You'll then find it very easy to keep a continual check on the length of every sentence while you are writing it.

A useful guide is that the warning lights should go on whenever a sentence gets longer than about 16 words (this actually had 20 words!).

This is because the average length of sentences in speeches is around eight seconds.

At about 120 words per minute this comes to 16 words.

The important word here is 'average', as there will be some sentences made up of fewer than 16 words, and some of more.

If the continuous monitoring of sentence length is to become a matter of routine, it's a good idea to get into the habit of using the same-sized font. Once you know where the words on the screen will be after 16 words, you will have a visual reminder of the point at which the sentence is in danger of becoming too long.

Visual Prompts

Starting each sentence on a new line not only enables you to monitor its length, but also makes its structure more visible than when the words are contained within a paragraph. Abandoning the paragraph is therefore one small step away from writing for the eyes of a reader, and a giant leap towards writing for the ears of an audience.

Seeing a line or two at a time makes it easier to look down, pick up the whole or part of a sentence, look up and deliver it. This becomes even easier when the print is much larger than is usual in most written material – though it's a mistake to think that typing the whole thing out in capital letters will help. The text of a speech, like that on road signs, will be much easier to read at a glance when printed in big lower-case letters.

The number of words on a line also has an effect on how easy it is to read from a text: the wider the line, the more difficult it becomes to scan it quickly. Like the choice of font size, the decision on column width will be very much a matter of personal preference, and it's a good idea to try out different options to discover which feels most comfortable.

You can make things even easier for yourself by marking up the text in advance. Single vertical slashes can be pencilled in to indicate a short pause, or double slashes for a longer one. Alternatively, the text can be laid out with the end of each line being a place to pause. Words to be given extra stress can be underlined or highlighted with a marker pen. Entering simple mood descriptions in the margins, such as 'seriously', 'ironically', 'assertively' and so on, can also provide effective reminders of changes in intonation and emphasis.

Creating The Visual Aids

The search for creative ways of getting points across should also include thinking about what visual aids (if any) you're likely to need. Leaving the decision about these until this fairly late stage in the preparation process has two major advantages:

1. You're likely to use far fewer visual aids than if you had opted for the traditional 'slides-first' approach to preparation.

2. You'll be selecting them to illustrate a particular point, rather than merely to remind you what to say next.

You're much less likely to make your audience suffer from slide fatigue than if your preparation had simply consisted of filling up a series of slides with bullet points. Your selection and design of visual aids should also be guided by the more detailed discussion in Step 3.

Rehearsal

A surprising number of speakers never bother to rehearse their talks beforehand. The importance of rehearsal is that it not only helps in estimating the timing of a speech or presentation, but also provides an opportunity to discover if any of it needs revising.

The more you go through something aloud, the more firmly fixed in your mind the words will become. It is not so much a matter of learning a speech off by heart as getting so familiar with what comes next in the overall structure that you become confident speaking from the notes or script. And, if you can recruit other people to listen to you rehearsing, you can get the benefit of useful feedback on how the audience is likely to react. Failing that, making an audio or video recording enables you to watch and evaluate your own performances. This will also help you to get over the initial dread of hearing yourself in public-speaking mode – before you actually deliver the speech.

Preparing For Question Time

Anticipating and preparing for questions is a fairly straightforward business. The following three-stage process has proved effective on numerous occasions. If possible, it's best to do it in a group: a few minds are always better than one, and are likely to generate more possibilities than when you try to do it on your own.

1. Brainstorm to produce a list of all the possible questions that you think might be raised by this particular audience.

2. Go through each question and work out the best possible way of answering it.

3. Having decided what to say, go one step further and think about how to get each point across in the most effective way (using, wherever possible, the techniques described in Step 4).

The importance of being well prepared and having a logical structure to your speech or presentation cannot be over-emphasised. It not only makes it much more likely that it will go down well with your audience, but has the added bonus of greatly reducing one of the main causes of the nervousness and lack of confidence that most people experience when speaking in public – being poorly prepared.

Step 2 Summary
Preparing, Planning and Structure

1. Analyse the audience:
   - Who's in the audience?
   - How big is it going to be?
   - What's the message for this audience?

2. Brainstorm the topic:
   - *Subjects:* Make a list of all the possible topics that could be included.
   - *Sectionalise:* Put the topics into sections.
   - *Sequence:* Reorder the sections into a logical sequence.

3. Create the structure:
   - *Pre-introduction* – to grab the attention of the audience.
   - *Introduction* – to let the audience know what you're going to be dealing with.
   - *Main body* – development of key messages.
   - *Summary* – brief restatement of main themes.
   - *Conclusion* – punchy line or two summing up most important message you want audience to take away.

4. Say it creatively
5. Create the visual aids
6. Rehearse, revise, rehearse
7. Prepare for question time (optional)

Step 3

Using Visual Aids

The acid test of a good visual aid is that it helps your audience's understanding or appreciation and is not there merely as a reminder for your benefit. Fortunately, the types of visuals that audiences like also happen to be ones that make it easier for you to communicate in a more natural and comfortable manner.

The Pitfalls Of Slides

Although heavy dependence on slides, mainly consisting of written bullet points, has become standard practice in many companies and organisations, this style of speaking causes more problems for audiences than most speakers realise.

Wordy Slides

Because projectors enable words and sentences to be projected on to a screen, the speaker doesn't have to give much thought to the style of language to be used, let alone what it's going to sound like to the audience. The fact that so many slides amount to little more than lists of prompts for the speaker also means that a lot of people don't bother to plan exactly what to say about each item, and end up making it up as they go along.

Another drawback is that projectors also enable large quantities of detailed material to be displayed on the screen. Here, speakers can fall into the trap of doing little or nothing to simplify and edit their content. As a result, preparation that begins and ends with writing a set of slides is almost certain to result in a presentation that inflicts massive information overload on the audience, expressed in language that's likely to come across as unduly technical, formal or just plain rambling.

Gazing Away Versus Gaining Attention

Slides work like magnets that draw people's eyes to the screen, beckoning them to look away from the speaker. Yet if eye contact is important for maintaining audience attention (*see Step 1*), why would anyone want to deflect the audience's attention away from them, especially at the start of a presentation?

The answer is that the risks associated with deflecting attention will outweigh the disadvantages only when you need to show the audience something that can't be easily communicated by words alone. Not surprisingly, then, the kinds of visual aid that audiences like best are those that help to clarify things for *them*, rather than ones that merely serve as a crutch for the speaker.

Reading, Listening or Neither

For members of an audience whose gaze has already shifted from speaker to screen, the sight of written words provides another distraction that divides and threatens their continued attentiveness. As soon as we see writing, we can't help reading it, or at least trying to read it. So the speaker is now asking us not only to break eye contact but also to use our brains to do two things at once – reading and listening – regardless of how difficult it is for anyone to do both at the same time.

Slides made up largely of writing also make things difficult for speakers. Some aren't sure whether to read them out word for word, or just leave them in the background for audiences to read at their leisure. Others announce a few moments of silence for people to read the slides for themselves. But just how long should you allow, and what are you supposed to do during the silence? Needless to say, none of these options impress audiences very much.

Build-up Rather Than Cover-up

In the days before overhead projectors gave way to PowerPoint*, audience reaction to speakers who used a sheet of paper to cover up the bullet points on a slide and then slid it down to reveal them one by one was generally negative. Yet ask the same people what they think about the computerised build-up of bullet points one by one, and the response is much more favourable.

The most likely reason for this is that it works in a similar way to the age-old practice of writing or drawing material on a blackboard, whiteboard or flip chart as you go along. And using a blackboard, whiteboard or flip chart is, of course, a well-tried medium with a long and distinguished track record.

Speaking from the Screen

Slide dependency causes problems for speakers as well as audiences. There are at least two main reasons why this style of delivery produces so few effective performances. First, because the presentation has been half-written out on the slides, speakers who haven't prepared what they are going to say about each bullet point have to improvise on the spot. And

* PowerPoint is a registered trademark of Microsoft Corporation.

only the quick-thinking and articulate few are able to avoid coming across as rambling and disjointed.

A second, and perhaps more fundamental, source of trouble is that speaking from notes projected on a screen is a style of communication that feels strange and unnatural, and adds another dimension to a speaker's sense of nervousness and unease.

Why Has The Slide-Driven Presentation Survived?

Ease and Convenience

One of the great attractions of the slide-driven approach is that it offers an easy way of appearing to be prepared and professional. The mere fact that you have some slides to show is enough in itself to qualify it as a 'proper' presentation in the eyes of audiences, who have been conditioned to expect nothing else.

Standardisation

Large corporations seized on the prospect of imposing a uniform and consistent message across different presentations by issuing standardised sets of slides to their workforce. But it showed little or no sensitivity for audiences who were condemned to listen to the presentations.

The 'No Notes' Illusion

Manufacturers of overhead projectors used to proclaim yet another alleged benefit of slide-dependent presentations: *with our machines, you can speak without having to use any notes*. This was an extraordinary claim on two counts. In the first place, they didn't free people from using notes: the only difference was that speakers stopped glancing down at their notes and started looking back at the screen to see what to say next. Secondly, it implied that there was something wrong or shameful about being seen to be using notes, in spite of the fact that, in all traditions of public speaking – whether preaching, lecturing, political speech-making or giving a best man's speech at a wedding – it is, and always has been, perfectly normal for speakers to use notes.

'Hard Copy of Slides Available Afterwards'

Slides seemed to hold out the advantage of people being able to take the notes away afterwards. But the knowledge that this is going to happen may actually reduce the audience's incentive to listen. And, as anyone who has ever been issued with such a pack will know, some go straight in the bin while others are filed away, never to be seen again.

Teaching Bad Habits

The rise of the slide-dependent presentation was speeded along by training programmes that were informed by observations of what more and more speakers were doing, without any attempt to find out how well or badly it was going down with audiences. But how many slide-driven presentations have you heard in which the speaker came across as really enthusiastic and inspiring? Having now posed this question to hundreds of people, I can report that most have to think quite hard to recall even a single instance, and no one has ever come up with a number higher than two.

Writing And Drawing While Speaking

Compared with speaking from lists on screens, there is something more natural about writing or drawing things on a board or flip chart. This traditional style of speaking also has a number of particular advantages over the slide-dependent model of presentation that has largely replaced it. It is important to know what these are, not only because you might like to try it out for yourself, but also because some of the advantages can be simulated or imitated by some of the functions in programs like PowerPoint.

Advantages of Using Boards and Flip Charts

Focus of Attention

Whereas slides divide the attention of the audience between looking at the speaker and looking at the screen, this is much less of a problem when you write or draw something on a board or flip chart. For obvious reasons, you're never more than an arm's length away from the thing you are inviting the audience to look at. Their focus of attention is therefore concentrated on a narrow visual field that includes both you and visual material.

Talking About what Everyone is Looking At

A second advantage of writing things up as you go along is that it makes it much easier to achieve better coordination between what you are saying and what you are asking the audience to look at. For example, while writing up a word, it's very easy to say the word at the same time. It's also easy to describe a drawing or diagram as you are drawing it.

Pace of Delivery

Perhaps the most important advantage of putting things on a board or flip chart as you go along is that the pace of your delivery will be more in tune with the pace at which audiences can comfortably take in new information. One of the problems with complex slides is that they suddenly confront audiences with far more information than can be taken in at a glance. But when writing or drawing, you have no choice but to lead the audience step-by-step through the point you are developing or explaining.

Dynamic Effects

Using boards and flip charts also opens up the opportunity to introduce elements of surprise that can make things more interesting for an audience. This can be something as simple as underlining or crossing out something you've already put on the board, or writing numbers into blank boxes on a pre-prepared table while talking about why they are interesting or significant. But it's also possible to simulate some of these advantages by using the animated functions in programs like PowerPoint. In fact, building up bullet points one by one is a quicker way of doing what speakers do when they write headings on a board. But you can also build graphs and charts up bit by bit, while giving a running commentary on what they show. At the click of a mouse, you can make graphs and charts appear on the screen, as if drawn by an invisible hand.

Spontaneity and Authority

Not all the advantages of using boards and flip charts can be simulated using computerised graphics. When you're writing or drawing in real time, there's an element of spontaneity and immediacy involved. From an audience point of view, whatever is being written or drawn is being done there and then for the sole benefit of everyone in the room – rather than a pre-packaged list or chart that was prepared in advance by your secretary, or circulated from head office. Speakers who put things up on a flip chart as they go along come across as being in full control of their material. It conveys an air of confidence, authority and command over the subject matter, something that is usually sadly lacking when a speaker has to depend on slides.

Even if you're afraid that you might forget what to put up on the board or flip chart, you can easily achieve an appearance of spontaneity and authority with a little advance planning and a light touch with a very fine pencil. Headings, numbers or diagrams can be drawn in or written up very faintly in advance, so that they are visible to you but not to the audience. All you have to do then is copy or trace the material at appropriate moments during the presentation, and the audience will marvel at your confident command over the subject.

Low Tech – High Impact

I know of no instance over the last 15 years in which someone who has tried using a board or flip chart has come to regret it. Speakers invariably report that they felt they had enjoyed much better rapport with their audiences and had received more positive feedback than when they had used slides.

Pitfalls to Avoid when Using Boards and Flip Charts

Writing Too Much or Too Slowly

Using a board or flip chart is, of course, not all plain sailing. If you write or draw too much on the chart at once, you run the risk of spending too long standing with your back to the audience. So it's important only to put up a little at a time, and to do so as quickly as possible. This means avoiding whole sentences and long words, and using shorthand where necessary.

Handwriting

Although people often worry about not having neat handwriting, this doesn't seem to bother audiences very much. If you plan to draw graphs or tables that include numbers or words, it's a good idea to draw in the axes or grids beforehand, which spares the audience from having to wait around watching your artistic efforts.

Dud Pens

A booby trap you need to be aware of is that many of the pens lined up along the bottom of flip charts and whiteboards have run out of ink. So it's a good idea to play safe by taking your own supply with you. Whenever possible, always use black or dark blue pens, reserving other colours for the occasional underlining or ringing of key points. This is because some colours, like green and red, are quite difficult to see from the back row. They can also cause problems for anyone in your audience who happens to be colour-blind.

The Visualiser

Although the use of boards and flip charts obviously works best in relatively small-scale settings where everyone in the audience can see what the speaker is showing them, the same results can be achieved by writing on rolls of acetate on an overhead projector. A more versatile development of this is the visualiser. This consists of a video camera pointing downwards from about the same height as the reflecting lens on an overhead projector. It will project more or less anything placed under it up on to the screen, whether it's a slide, picture or even a page from a book. On one occasion I saw a speaker, equipped with nothing more than a visualiser, a felt-tip pen and a few sheets of A4 paper, receive a rapturous response from an audience of 800 people.

Visual Aids That Audiences Like

Audiences are not averse to *all* kinds of slides. In fact, one of the biggest – and as yet under-used – advantages of computerised graphics is the ease with which you can create professional-looking pictorial images. As we shall see below, it is the *genuinely visual* visual aids that audiences like the best.

The biggest plus of programs like PowerPoint is that they not only make it possible to capitalise on some of the advantages of writing on a board or flip chart, but also have tremendous potential for generating the kinds of visual aids that audiences like, such as pictorial images. On the minus side, some of PowerPoint's templates positively encourage speakers to produce the types of slide and presentation that are least likely to impress audiences, such as ones featuring complicated tables and large quantities of written material.

Objects, Props and Demonstrations

A vivid image from the UK general election of 1979 was a picture of Margaret Thatcher using a pair of scissors to cut a pound note in two. Inflation was a major issue in the campaign, and this was her way of showing how much the currency had suffered during the preceding years of Labour government.

Holding up an object while referring to it can be enough to strike a chord with an audience. In the context of a business presentation it might be something as simple as a report, a proposal or a handout that is going to be distributed afterwards. But the scope for using objects and props to illustrate a point is more or less infinite.

Demonstrations, ranging from scientific experiments to home-made jam-making, have always been an effective way of showing people how to do things that are complicated and difficult to describe in abstract terms. But, as with all visual aids, there are some potential pitfalls.

Avoid Gimmicks

Audiences tend not to be very impressed by the use of objects that are not obviously relevant to the point being made, especially if they appear too gimmicky, or are being used purely for the sake of livening up an otherwise boring presentation.

Plan and Practise

If you are to avoid embarrassing disasters, careful planning and practice are needed. Audiences quickly lose confidence if your demonstrations fail to work, or if you seem unsure when handling your props.

Don't Distribute

Don't be tempted to pass an object around for people to inspect for themselves, as it will only distract their attention away from you and what you are saying – and you might never get it back!

Pictures

Some of the best talks I ever attended were by an art teacher who revelled in talking us through slides of famous paintings, and an inspired Women's Institute lecturer, who used sets of colour transparencies to illustrate her talks on the dry stone walls of the Lake District. The key to both these speakers' success was that they understood the need for careful selection of the slides, and equally careful advance preparation of the accompanying commentary.

Editing Pictures

The first priority in using pictures must always be ruthless editing to ensure that the picture vividly illustrates the point. As for how many slides you should use per minute, or for a five- or ten-minute presentation, the answer could be one or twenty-one, depending on the point you want to get across. I once saw a doctor give a brilliant 15-minute talk on a particular illness, in which his only visual aid was one slide showing a simplified picture of the internal organs of the human body. On another occasion, I saw an architect show 20 pictures of different buildings in not much more than a minute. The doctor needed to be able to point to various details on the picture from time to time during his presentation; the architect wanted to give his audience a general impression of what his buildings looked like.

Clipart and Cartoons

As with objects and props, it's important not to use pictures just for the sake of it. This has become an ever-present temptation thanks to the huge libraries of clipart images built into so many software packages. A related hazard is the cartoon, which seldom has any impact other than to give the impression that the speaker is taking a desperate measure to liven things up. So think carefully before including them, or play safe and leave them out altogether.

Looking for Pictorial Possibilities

As long as pictures are relevant to the subject matter, they can usually be relied on to go down well with audiences. It's therefore a good idea to be continually on the lookout for illustrative material that you might be able to use. Some things that may not seem obviously pictorial in the first place can often make more of an impact by being turned into pictures. For example, when referring to clients to whom your company has supplied goods or services, a slide made up of familiar corporate logos is a much more vivid way of conveying the general impression you want to make than a boring list of names.

Video and DVD

When using video to illustrate a point, it's usually best to keep the clips short. The 30-second television commercial is a useful guide to optimal length. If you play longer clips, the danger is that the audience will start to feel as though they are at a film show rather than a presentation. Once that happens, you may well find yourself losing the impetus, and have problems getting them back into the mood for listening to a talk. And, if it is a lively and well-produced piece of video, there's the added risk of coming across as dull and amateurish compared with what they've just been watching.

Maps

If your aim is to give an overall impression of something like the number of branches and/or their geographical coverage, the obvious solution is to use a simple map with towns or countries marked on it. And if you're going to discuss each place in more detail, you can use programs like PowerPoint to bring the place names up one by one, which prevents the audience from being distracted by other locations that you have not yet talked about.

Organisation Charts

If you must use them, keep them clear and simple and maintain interest by building up the different levels one by one. However, before describing an organisation at all, it's always worth giving some serious thought to just how interesting or relevant such information is likely to be to the audience. It is very common for speakers who are presenting to prospective clients to start with a detailed description of the company, its mission statement, corporate values and so on. It's also common for prospective clients, who may have to listen to several similar presentations in a single morning, to become quite impatient about having to endure yet another one.

Diagrams and Flow Charts

When it comes to discussing complex arrangements, processes or theoretical models, various kinds of diagram come into their own. But, as with organisation charts, make sure you keep them simple.

Graphs

The most frequent use of numbers in presentations is to show trends, relationships and proportions, all of which can be depicted much more effectively in graphical form than with raw numbers. Graphs, bar charts and pie charts all get higher ratings from audiences than tables of numbers – but only if you keep them simple and explain them clearly as you introduce them. Some PowerPoint templates use such thin lines and faint colours that they are hardly visible even from a short distance away from the screen. It is therefore worth learning how to replace them with thicker lines and stronger colours.

Bar Charts

Audiences also tend to react positively to the use of bar charts when listening to discussions of various types of numerical data. On the PowerPoint template, the bars stand out more clearly than the wispy lines on some of its graphs, but some of the fonts are too small to ensure visibility from the back row. The audience also has the problem of trying to make instant sense of the twelve bars, three different colours and four periods of time depicted on one of the standard templates.

Many speakers assume that the contents of such charts will be instantly accessible to an audience.

They launch straight into a discussion of the figures as soon as the chart goes up on the screen, without bothering to say anything about what the axes, bars and colours actually represent. You can show greater sensitivity to the audience's needs by exploiting other functions within PowerPoint to adapt charts to make them simpler and easier to understand. The program also lets you add bars one by one, so that you can get the audience to focus on one set of figures at a time before revealing the next one – and so on until the chart is complete.

Pie Charts

Proportions are best illustrated by pie charts as long as, again, they are kept as simple as possible. The basic PowerPoint template passes the simplicity test, but it also brings with it the temptation to slice the pies into so many segments that they end up being too complicated to mean much to anyone. And, unless you really want to confuse your audience, avoid the temptation to put up more than one pie chart at the same time, and certainly don't try to break the record number I've seen so far of eight pie charts on a single slide!

Blanking out the Screen: A Non-visual Exception

If there is something on the screen, even if it's only your corporate logo, audiences have a reason to look away and break eye contact with the speaker. One way to prevent this is to insert a slide that is completely blank. With PowerPoint, all you have to do is apply a black background to a slide, and it will appear to the audience as though there is nothing on the screen at all. Or you can create the same effect by pressing the relevant function key on your computer. A blank screen also ensures that you have the audience's full attention at the beginning and end of presentations.

Handouts: A Textual Exception

Although all presentations should aim to simplify the content as much as possible, there are some subjects where it's difficult to avoid dealing with detailed material altogether. A speaker might, for example, need to take an audience through financial or other statistical data. In such instances you have to make a choice between projecting the numbers onto a screen and printing them out on handouts for distributing around the room.

There are two common fears associated with handouts. The first is that everyone will start reading; and the second is that the resulting loss of eye contact will divert the audience from listening to what you are saying. A partial solution to the first of these is not to hand anything out until you're ready to start talking about it. Once they get a copy in their hands, people will, of course, start reading it. So you have to move quickly to take control, firmly directing their attention to the first detail to be discussed. This will typically involve telling them to look at the first example or whatever detail you want to start with. You will then become aware of a sudden and complete loss of eye contact with the audience, which, under other circumstances, would be cause for serious panic. But when using a handout, it's a promising sign that you've engaged the audience's attention on what you want to discuss. And it's even more encouraging if they seem interested enough to start writing notes on the handouts.

The Potential And Pitfalls Of PowerPoint

PowerPoint Plus Points

Pictures
It makes it extremely easy to incorporate photographs and other types of picture into a presentation. These can be used in just the same way as 35mm projectors were used in traditional slide shows.

Graphics

It provides great scope for producing graphs, charts, diagrams and all the other types of pictorial material that audiences find useful – though you do have to be prepared to simplify and modify the templates if necessary.

Build-up

The capacity to build up bullet points and animate charts enables you to simulate using a flip chart or board, and benefit from some of the advantages (as discussed earlier, *page 62*). But play safe by using the simpler options, such as 'appear' or 'wipe down', as some of the more exotic possibilities can be very distracting for an audience. These include bullet points that come swivelling or swooping in from all corners of the slide (sometimes accompanied by the sound of gunfire, screeching brakes or breaking glass).

Slide Changing

The ease with which you can change slides at the push of a button makes for much smoother transitions than the shuffling of acetates (with its associated delays and distractions).

PowerPoint Minus Points

In my experience, most non-expert PowerPoint users appreciate their slides being neater and more professional looking, but have a number of reservations. They would love to make more use of pictures and charts, but only know how to create slides made up of lists; they would like to use the build-up and animated functions, but haven't yet worked out how to do it. And those who do have the necessary expertise often say that they would make even more use of such slides if only it didn't take so much time to design and prepare them. None of these problems would arise if the templates built into PowerPoint made it easier for users to generate the types of pictorial and dynamic visuals that audiences actually find useful.

Bias Towards Detail

Some of PowerPoint's default fonts, lines and colours tend to be too small or too faint to be easily seen from a distance. And some of the basic templates implicitly invite users to overload their slides with far more information than audiences can comfortably take in at a glance.

Bias Towards Written Words and Lists

An even stronger incentive to create textual slides is built into the collection of 24 model presentations that come as part of the package. Leaving aside the one for a website, the remaining 23 presentations include a total of 214 slides, of which the overwhelming majority (94 per cent) consist of nothing but text, at an average of 20 words per slide. A further two slides (1 per cent) feature tables with words and columns of raw numbers. The vast majority are therefore indistinguishable from the static lists of bullet points that have been the norm since the days of acetates and overhead projectors. They also exhibit an extraordinary reluctance on the part of Microsoft's designers to use one of the most positive features of their own software – the build-up function – which makes an appearance in only one of the 23 sets of model presentations.

Bias Against Pictures and Charts

Of the remaining 5 per cent of specimen slides that actually include some of the types of visuals that audiences find most useful, there are two graphs, one bar chart, two pie charts and eight diagrams. Of these, only the two pie charts (1 per cent of the total collection) appear on their own with minimal text to distract the audience's attention. But the single example of a bar chart assumes that audiences will have no difficulties in taking in three of them at the same time.

The other visual slides include text above, below, to the side of or within the graphical images. So, as a model of how to make the most of the graphical and pictorial capabilities of PowerPoint, they provide little guidance on the creation of simple, uncluttered visual slides that are most likely to help speakers get their points across.

PowerPoint: Use with Caution!

Short of a massive overhaul of the program, releasing the positive potential of PowerPoint can only be done by approaching it with caution, and a willingness to modify some of its standard templates. That means rejecting its in-built bias towards heavily textual slides, and learning how to simplify its graphs, charts and diagrams. It's also worth making an effort to master its other pictorial and dynamic capabilities, and especially some of its build-up and animated functions.

Life After Death From 1,000 Slides

At first sight, it might seem that to abandon the industry-standard model of slide presentation is far too radical a step to take. But the good news is that, once people get over their dependence on textual slides in favour of visual aids that are more sensitive to the needs and preferences of audiences, they immediately experience better rapport with their listeners. Visual aids prepared with the audience in mind also greatly reduce the chances of inflicting too much information on the listener. Taken together, these represent an important move towards mastering the language of public speaking.

The next challenge is to find an escape route from the boring language that typically adorns the word-filled slide, and from the dull, dislocated and *ad hoc* commentaries it tends to prompt from speakers.

Step 3 Summary
Using Visual Aids

1. Using slides effectively:
   - Use as few words as possible on slides.
   - Don't distract audiences by inviting them to read and listen at the same time.
   - If you do put bullet points on a slide, plan what to say about each one.
   - Build bullet points up one at a time.
   - Don't spend too much time looking at the screen.
   - Don't block the audience's view by standing between them and the screen.
   - Get used to the equipment beforehand.

2. Advantages of writing and drawing while speaking:
   - Focus of attention remains on you.
   - The talk and visual material are coordinated.
   - Pace of delivery is better for the audience.
   - It gives you an air of spontaneity and authority.

3. Disadvantages of writing and drawing while speaking:
   - Writing too much or too slowly.
   - Felt-tip pens that run out of ink.
   - Some colours can't be seen clearly at a distance.

4. Visual aids that go down well with audiences:
- Objects, props and demonstrations
- Pictures
- Video
- Maps
- Organisation charts
- Graphs
- Bar charts
- Pie charts
- Non-visual exceptions: blank slides (such as a black background); handouts

5. PowerPoint plus points:
- Pictures and video
- Graphics
- Build-up
- Slide changing

6. PowerPoint minus points:
- Encourages too much detail
- Tempts users to produce lists
- Discourages build-up
- Discourages pictures and charts
- Endorses slide-dependent presentations

Step 4

Inspiring Your Audience

Is there anything you can do to get messages across with greater impact? Are there any particular techniques that successful speakers use to inspire, persuade and enthuse their audiences? And can anyone learn to use them to become more effective communicators? The answer to all these questions is an emphatic *YES*.

In fact, the techniques described here were originally identified by the ancient Greeks, but are still very much alive and well today. They are part and parcel of the way all effective speakers speak, and are to be heard in action wherever people are arguing, and whenever someone is trying to be persuasive or convincing. Compare the alternatives in options A and B overleaf. Each means more or less the same, but you'll see at a glance that one version is rather more striking than the other:

Option A	Option B
I can't decide whether or not to commit suicide.	To be, or not to be. **Shakespeare (Hamlet)**
Nobody is going to make me change my economic policies.	You turn if you want to. The lady's not for turning. **Margaret Thatcher**
I hope that racial discrimination in America will disappear within a generation.	I have a dream that one day my four little children will one day live in a nation where they will not be judged by the colour of their skin, but by the content of their character. **Martin Luther King**

You may have noticed that all of them involve the use of a contrast – between 'you turning' and 'the lady not turning', between 'to be' and 'not to be', and between 'the colour of their skin' and 'the content of their character'. As such, they are famous examples of the use of the first type of timeless technique you need to know about to get your points across with greater impact.

The Timeless Toolkit

Contrasts

For at least 2,000 years, many of the quotations that have survived have involved the use of a contrast:

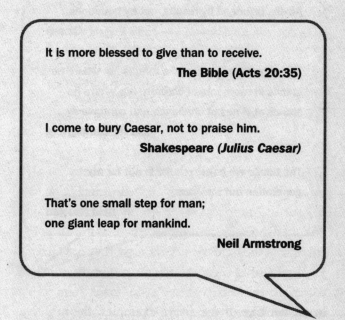

It is more blessed to give than to receive.
The Bible (Acts 20:35)

I come to bury Caesar, not to praise him.
Shakespeare (*Julius Caesar*)

That's one small step for man;
one giant leap for mankind.
Neil Armstrong

Although all these statements make a contrast between two things, they do so in rather different ways, and it is important to know what some of the most common and adaptable forms are.

Contradictions: 'Not This but That'

Simple though it may seem, following a negative with a positive, or vice versa, has a very impressive history when it comes to summing up points in a punchy way:

> Advice is judged by results, not by intentions.
>
> **Cicero**
>
> The ultimate measure of a man is not where he stands in moments of comfort, but where he stands at times of challenge and controversy.
>
> **Martin Luther King**
>
> The house we hope to build is not for my generation but for yours.
>
> **Ronald Reagan**

In all but one of the above examples, the negative comes before the positive, and this is by far the commonest form of contradictory contrast. But if the speaker wants the audience to focus on the negative, as with Margaret Thatcher's 'You turn if you want to. The lady's not for turning', the positive will come first.

Comparisons: 'More This Than That'

Language gives us tools for making comparative statements so that we can contrast one thing as being 'more than', 'better than', 'bigger than' something else:

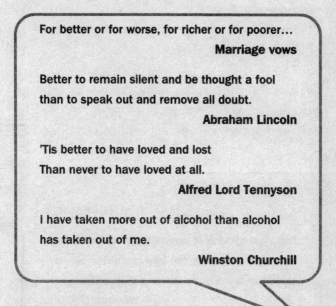

> For better or for worse, for richer or for poorer...
> **Marriage vows**
>
> Better to remain silent and be thought a fool than to speak out and remove all doubt.
> **Abraham Lincoln**
>
> 'Tis better to have loved and lost
> Than never to have loved at all.
> **Alfred Lord Tennyson**
>
> I have taken more out of alcohol than alcohol has taken out of me.
> **Winston Churchill**

Opposites: 'Black or White'

'Good' and 'evil' and 'life' and 'death' are examples of the many hundreds of words that have directly opposite meanings. The range is vast, and is not confined to any particular parts of speech. For example:

Nouns: truth-falsehood, happiness-misery, health-illness, etc.

Verbs: attack-defend, live-die, sit-stand, etc.

Adjectives: kind-cruel, hot-cold, bright-dull, etc.

Adverbs: always-never, quickly-slowly, honestly-dishonestly, etc.

Prepositions: up-down, before-after, above-below, etc.

The fact that there are so many words with opposite meanings provides immense scope for producing stark and dramatic-sounding contrasts:

> Fair is foul, and foul is fair.
>
> **Shakespeare (*Macbeth*)**
>
> The inherent vice of capitalism is the unequal sharing of blessings; the inherent virtue of socialism is the equal sharing of miseries.
>
> **Winston Churchill**
>
> There is nothing wrong with America that cannot be solved by what's right with America.
>
> **Bill Clinton**

Phrase Reversals

There is a particularly elegant type of contrast, in which some of the same words in the first part of the contrast are turned around in the second part:

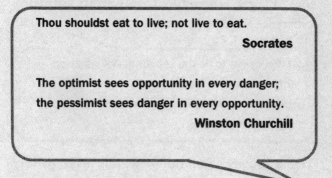

Thou shouldst eat to live; not live to eat.

Socrates

The optimist sees opportunity in every danger;
the pessimist sees danger in every opportunity.

Winston Churchill

The reversal of key words in the second part of a contrast was used in some of the most widely quoted lines from US President Kennedy's inaugural speech:

Ask not what your country can do for you;
ask what you can do for your country.

Let us never negotiate out of fear.
But let us never fear to negotiate.

John F. Kennedy

Repetition, Balance and Anticipation

The two parts of most memorable contrasts are not only of similar length, but also sound very similar. An extreme case of this form of repetition came in Tony Blair's last leader's speech to his party conference in 2006:

> I don't want to be the Labour leader who won three successive elections.
> I want to be the first Labour leader to win three successive elections.

From a listener's point of view, this makes it very easy to notice the elements that change, and to instantly get the point. If, as at political rallies, the audience is on the lookout for a slot where they can applaud, the first part of a contrast provides listeners with a fairly obvious clue as to when the second part of the contrast will come to an end, and when the applause can start.

Puzzles and Questions

Puzzle-solution Formats

The first part of a contrast typically poses an implicit puzzle that gets the audience wondering what the solution will be – if it's not one thing, what is it? But you don't need to make a contrast to say something that prompts listeners to start trying to anticipate a solution, rather in the same way as good writing will make readers want to see what is on the next page. If you increase their attentiveness to a point where they will be listening closely for what comes next, your solution is likely to get a positive response, especially if it is humorous or witty, as when Ronald Reagan declared his candidacy for the Republican presidential nomination in 1980:

> PUZZLE: This is a moment of quite some mixed emotions for me.
>
> SOLUTION: I haven't been on prime-time television for quite a while.
>
> **Ronald Reagan**

After he had become president, something Ronald Reagan had done was used by a former British prime minister to pose a puzzle:

> PUZZLE: Then President Reagan did a very wise thing.
>
> SOLUTION: He dismissed all the academic economists in Washington.
>
> **Harold Macmillan**

In both these sequences, the solutions to the puzzles prompted laughter and applause, and showed how the technique can be used for humorous purposes. But puzzles can also be used to focus the audience's attention on a more serious message that's about to be delivered:

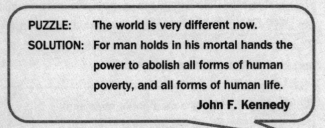

PUZZLE: The world is very different now.
SOLUTION: For man holds in his mortal hands the
                  power to abolish all forms of human
                  poverty, and all forms of human life.

John F. Kennedy

Questions with Answers

The simplest and commonest type of puzzle is to ask the audience a question or series of questions. Even though members of an audience know that they are not actually going to have to give an answer, it will still make them sit up and start wondering what's coming next.

What is conservatism?
Is it not the adherence to the old and tried
against the new and untried?

Abraham Lincoln

One of the most common uses of rhetorical questions is for making a link from a section that has just been completed to the one that's coming next:

> **So much for the past.**
> **What about the future?**
> **So much for the problems.**
> **What solutions can we offer?**

Some people worry that to ask a question is to risk being interrupted by a heckler. This hardly ever happens because most members of an audience know that any question they hear requires no immediate response from them.

Lists of Three

Another technique that regularly triggers applause in political speeches is the three-part list. This features in many famous quotations. It can be made up of:

Three identical words:

> **No, no, no. Margaret Thatcher**
>
> **Education, education, education. Tony Blair**

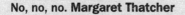

Three different words:

> I am the way, the truth and the light.
>
> **New Testament**
>
> Liberté, egalité, fraternité.
>
> **French revolutionary slogan**

Three phrases:

> Government of the people by the people for the people.
>
> **Abraham Lincoln**
>
> I stand before you today the representative of a family in grief, in a country in mourning before a world in shock.
>
> **Lord Spencer (at Princess Diana's funeral)**

Three clauses:

> Happiness is when what you think, what you say, and what you do are in harmony.
>
> **Mahatma Gandhi**
>
> Strengthened by their courage, heartened by their valour and borne by their memory, let us continue to stand for the ideals for which they lived and died.
>
> **Ronald Reagan**

Three sentences:

> The time for the healing of the wounds has come.
> The moment to bridge the chasms that divide us
> has come.
> The time to build is upon us.
>
> **Nelson Mandela**

Giving the Impression of Completeness

One of the attractions of three-part lists is that they create an impression of completeness. Lists with only two items in them sound inadequate, and hardly seem to constitute a proper list, while lists of four items or more are more difficult for an audience to take in.

Putting the Longest Item Last

An intriguing feature of many well-known three-part lists is that they have a third item that is longer than the first two. This can take the form of longer words, or more words in third position, as in the following examples:

> Father, Son and Holy Spirit.
>
> **New Testament**
>
> The inalienable right to life, liberty and the pursuit of happiness.
>
> **American Declaration of Independence**
>
> I swear to tell the truth, the whole truth and nothing but the truth.
>
> **Courtroom oath**

If your third point is the most important of the three, making it longer is a simple way of highlighting its greater significance compared with the first two. It also requires the audience to spend more time listening to the third point than to each of the earlier ones.

Combined Formats

In the example on page 95, Tony Blair's repetition of the word 'education' was actually prefaced by a question that announced that his answer would come in three parts. As such, it combined two techniques – the puzzle-solution format and a three-part list – in the same sequence:

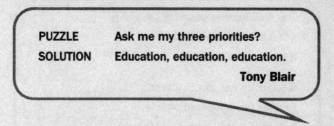

PUZZLE   Ask me my three priorities?
SOLUTION Education, education, education.

Tony Blair

This is an example of how different techniques can be combined in different ways, and brings us to one of the most important weapons in the speaker's armoury: the combined format.

Combining for Greater Impact

If the use of a single technique to package a message has a positive impact on an audience, using more than one at the same time tends to prompt longer and louder bursts of applause than normal. This way of combining techniques appears to be used more frequently by politicians with reputations as outstanding orators, such as Winston Churchill and Martin Luther King, than by the more average, run-of-the mill speaker.

There are a number of different ways in which the various techniques can be combined.

Lists of three contrasts

Speakers don't have to stop at using one contrast, but can produce several in a row:

> The new frontier of which I speak is
> not a set of promises
> it is a set of challenges.
>
> It sums up not what I intend
> to offer the American people,
> but what I intend to ask of them.
>
> It appeals to their pride,
> not their pocketbook.
>
> **John F. Kennedy**

Puzzle posed by second part of a contrast

The second part of the following contrast poses a puzzle that is then solved by a list of three. Coming as it did exactly 10 years after the speech in which the original quote appeared, it is also a nice example of how something as simple as repeating the same word three times can survive long after it was first delivered.

> [A]   Tony Blair once told us that his
> priorities could be summed up in
> three words: education,
> education, education.
> [B] [PUZZLE]   I can do mine in three letters:
> [SOLUTION]   N - H - S.
>
> **David Cameron**

Lists of questions

Posing one rhetorical question after another can also build up an audience's sense of anticipation, as was done very effectively in Ronald Reagan's speech to veterans on the 40th anniversary of the Normandy landings:

> ... you risked everything here. Why? Why did you do it? What impelled you to put aside the instinct for self-preservation and risk your lives to take these cliffs? What inspired all the men of the armies that met here? We look at you, and somehow we know the answer. It was faith and belief; it was loyalty and love.
>
> **Ronald Reagan**

Combining lists and contrasts

Sometimes the first part of the contrast can be made up of three items, as in the following example:

> When I was a child, I spake as a child, I understood as a child, I thought as a child; but when I became a man, I put away childish things.
>
> **St Paul, 1 Corinthians 13:11**

Puzzle with contrasting solution

One way of solving a puzzle is with a solution in the form of a contrast, as when Winston Churchill explained how difficult it is to make an after-dinner speech:

> **PUZZLE** There are two things that are more difficult than making an after-dinner speech:
>
> **SOLUTION** climbing a wall which is leaning toward you and kissing a girl who is leaning away from you.
>
> **Winston Churchill**

Puzzle with solutions in three parts

Solutions to puzzles can also come in three parts, as in:

> **PUZZLE** There are three kinds of lies.
>
> **SOLUTION** Lies, damned lies, and statistics.
>
> **Benjamin Disraeli**

Three-part lists where each item contrasts with the one before it

It can also be very effective to contrast a second item with the first, and the third one with the second:

> You can fool some of the people all of the time,
> and all of the people some of the time, but you
> cannot fool all of the people all of the time.
>
> **Abraham Lincoln**
>
> This is not the end.
> It is not even the beginning of the end.
> But it is perhaps the end of the beginning.
>
> **Winston Churchill**

Three-part lists with a third item that contrasts with the first two

A very simple and adaptable technique that can be used to get almost any key point across is to contrast a third item with the first two:

> I am not an Athenian
> or a Greek,
> but a citizen of the world.
>
> **Socrates**
>
> ... we pledge our best efforts to help them help themselves...
> not because the Communists may be doing it,
> not because we seek their votes,
> but because it is right.
>
> **John F. Kennedy**

All a speaker has to do is start by deciding what the main point to be made is, and then find two negatives to go in front of it (or, if the point is in the negative, two positives):

> We will negotiate for it [peace],
> sacrifice for it,
> we will never surrender for it, now or ever.
>
> **Ronald Reagan**

The same technique is to be found in large numbers of jokes, where the punchline comes in third position. What makes them funny is that the third point contrasts with the expectation established by the first two parts. As in:

> ... freedom of speech,
> freedom of conscience,
> and the prudence never to practise either.
>
> **Mark Twain**

So far, we have concentrated on ways of putting words, phrases and sentences together that have a long and well-proven record of striking chords with audiences. Next, we look at another very important set of techniques with just as long and distinguished a history.

Painting Pictures With Words

It's often said that a picture can paint a thousand words. But words can just as easily be used to create a thousand images. Whether it's '*an iron curtain descending*' across Europe (Winston Churchill), '*a wind of change blowing*' across Africa (Harold Macmillan) or '*a great beacon light of hope shining*' across America (Martin Luther King), we know instantly that the speaker is not speaking literally, and have no trouble in seeing exactly what is meant.

A single word, phrase or sentence can often be enough to get across a point that would otherwise take many more sentences to explain. Imagery can also be seen as another type of contrast, as it involves making an implicit or explicit comparison between a particular image and the actual subject matter under discussion.

Everyday Imagery

An ability to use imagery effectively is not a specialised art that is a monopoly of great speakers or writers, but is a thoroughly normal and regular feature of everyday speech. In fact, many images are so much a part of the language that we are hardly even aware that we are speaking metaphorically. We sometimes *bite off more than we can chew*, find things *as easy as pie*, sleep *like a log*, or run *like the wind.* There are those who *live in the fast lane* and *spend an arm and a leg* on maintaining their lifestyle, while others *live from hand to mouth* without *two pennies to rub together.*

Although everyone may be perfectly at ease using imagery in everyday speech, many speakers don't carry on using it when addressing an audience. In the case of business presentations, it's as if people feel that they have to speak in a much more official and analytical way than usual, and must therefore avoid using anything that smacks of colourful language. What they don't realise is that something that all effective speakers have in common is a capacity to use imagery in interesting and imaginative ways. Nor should it be thought that you have to avoid imagery when speaking analytically about facts and information. Even the language of science and technology is littered with metaphors and analogies. Magnetic *fields*, sound *waves* and *cells* have been with us for generations, and we now think nothing of using search *engines*, *robots* and *spiders* to *surf the net*, *navigating our way* through an information *superhighway* in *cyberspace*, using computers that are vulnerable to *infections* from *viruses*, *worms* and *Trojans.*

Types of Imagery

Similes (explicit comparisons using the word 'like')

Sometimes called 'open' or 'overt' comparisons, similes make it clear that the thing being talked about is *like* something else:

> My love is like a red, red rose
> That's newly sprung in June:
> My love is like the melodie
> That's sweetly played in tune.
>
> **Robert Burns**
>
> I'll be floating like a butterfly and stinging like a bee.
>
> **Muhammad Ali**

But similes can just as easily be used to criticise or poke fun at someone:

> Being attacked by Sir Geoffrey Howe is like being savaged by a dead sheep.
>
> **Denis Healey (former British Chancellor of the Exchequer)**

You can also use similes in combination with the techniques discussed earlier, as in the following example of three in a row:

> A hippie is someone who walks like Tarzan,
> looks like Jane and smells like Cheetah.
>
> **Ronald Reagan**

There is considerable scope for using them to set up the first part of a puzzle-solution sequence:

> Being powerful is like being a lady.
> If you have to tell people you are, you aren't.
>
> **Margaret Thatcher**

Whereas similes make it quite clear that one thing is being compared with another, metaphors achieve similar effects in a rather less obvious way.

Metaphors (implicit comparisons using words that literally mean something else)

Metaphor involves using a comparative image without using words like 'as' or 'like' to make it explicit that this is what you are doing; it leaves it to listeners to get the point for themselves. This may only involve a word or two, as in various famous insults and nicknames: Churchill referred to Mussolini as 'the bullfrog of the Pontine marshes'; Margaret Thatcher was variously described as 'the iron lady', 'Attila the Hen' and the 'immaculate misconception'; according to Gore Vidal, Ronald Reagan was 'a triumph of the embalmer's art'. These examples highlight something every schoolchild knows and every teacher fears, namely that nicknames based on metaphors that sum up some particular characteristic of a person tend to stick.

But metaphors are just as useful for paying people compliments, as when we talk of someone being a 'tower of strength' or 'solid as a rock', and there is an almost infinite scope for using similes and metaphors to get almost any point across. But you don't always have to stop after a few words or sentences, and can sometimes expand on them in greater detail.

Analogies (or parallels)

Margaret Thatcher revelled in making parallels between the management of the British economy and her experience as a housewife managing a domestic budget. More generally, analogies are widely used in the teaching of science and medicine. Discussions of electricity often use the analogy of water flowing through pipes; in medicine the heart can be thought of as a pump, the liver as a filter, and so on.

You can sometimes successfully extend analogies to develop more serious themes at greater length. One of the most outstanding exponents of this was

Martin Luther King. Among famous orators, his mastery of metaphor and analogy was second to none, as can be seen by reading almost any of his major speeches. Cashing a cheque at a bank might seem at first sight to be a rather unpromising analogy, but he managed to develop it in a way that vividly summed up the issues that had given rise to the civil rights movement.

> ... America has given the Negro people a *bad cheque which has come back marked 'insufficient funds'*. But we refuse to believe that the *bank of justice is bankrupt*. We refuse to believe that there are *insufficient funds in the great vaults of opportunity* of this nation. *So we have come to cash this cheque – a cheque that will give us upon demand the riches of freedom* and the security of justice. We have also come to this *hallowed* spot to remind America of the fierce urgency of now.
>
> **Martin Luther King**

Mixing and Modifying Metaphors

Care is needed when extending an image because it is easy for speakers to confuse one metaphor with another without realising it.

> **Security is the essential *roadblock* to achieving the *road map to peace*.**
>
> **George W. Bush**

The result can be amusing for listeners, even though this may not be what the speaker was intending.

But in the case of metaphors that are so well known that everyone has heard of them, you can sometimes modify them to get a point across in a humorous way:

> **Every silver lining has a cloud.**
>
> **Anonymous**
>
> **He was born with a silver foot in his mouth.**
>
> **Ann Richards (about George Bush Sr)**

Similar witty effects can be achieved by extending famous metaphors, as in:

> **Familiarity breeds contempt – and children.**
>
> **Mark Twain**
>
> **A stitch in time would have confused Einstein.**
>
> **Anonymous**

Anecdotes

When it comes to speaking in public – whether teaching a class, preaching a sermon, making a political or after-dinner speech or giving a business presentation – people with reputations as effective speakers invariably excel at using illustrative anecdotes to get key points across. In fact, it can be such an effective technique that I have often thought large organisations ought to employ corporate anthropologists, whose job would be to collect stories about successes and failures that could be used to liven up management presentations.

The two key rules for the effective use of anecdotes are, first, that they should be relevant to the point being made; and, second, that they should not go on for too long. The trouble is that being brief and to the point is easier said than done, and requires you to be very disciplined about what details to include or exclude. The parable of the Good Samaritan, for example, is one of the most famous anecdotes of all times, and, consisting of a mere 166 words, is a model of economy.

A more recent master of the well-chosen anecdote was Ronald Reagan, who had the knack of fitting them perfectly to the occasion and the audience. His address to Second World War veterans on the 40th anniversary of the Normandy landings included the following:

Do you remember the story of Bill Millin of the 51st Highlanders? Forty years ago today, British troops were pinned down near a bridge, waiting desperately for help. Suddenly, they heard the sound of bagpipes, and some thought they were dreaming. Well, they weren't. They looked up and saw Bill Millin with his bagpipes, leading the reinforcements and ignoring the smack of bullets into the ground around him. Lord Lovat was with him – Lord Lovat of Scotland – who calmly announced when he got to the bridge, 'Sorry, I'm a few minutes late,' as if he'd been delayed by a traffic jam, when in truth he'd just come from the bloody fighting on Sword Beach, which he and his men had just taken.

Ronald Reagan

I have included this anecdote in full to underline the point that the most effective storytellers keep them brief. Although it's difficult to be precise about the perfect length, the evidence from famous speeches that both had an impact when delivered and were remembered years later is that the most effective anecdotes hardly ever take much more than a minute to deliver.

The Sound of Words

Before the invention of writing, imagery and storytelling were used to store and pass on ideas and information in a purely spoken form. Just as important, especially when it comes to remembering poems, is the sound of the words themselves and the part played by things like alliteration, rhythm and rhymes.

Used in moderation, alliteration – in which a series of words start with the same sound – is the most adaptable of these when it comes to making speeches:

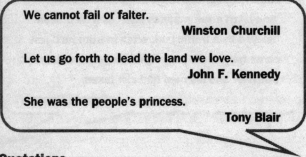

We cannot fail or falter.
Winston Churchill

Let us go forth to lead the land we love.
John F. Kennedy

She was the people's princess.
Tony Blair

Quotations

Many of the examples of similes, metaphors and analogies referred to in this chapter are to be found in dictionaries of quotations, which are widely used by speakers as a source of inspiration. They provide a rich resource, not only of imagery that might be worth borrowing and re-using, but also of lines suitable for quoting verbatim during a speech or presentation. As with other forms of imagery, the main rule in selecting a quotation is that it should be relevant to the point you want to get across.

Naturally Gifted Speakers?

Almost all the examples mentioned so far have been taken from famous speakers or writers from different periods of history. The advantage of using well-known sources is that it underlines the fact that all persuasive speakers, regardless of their nationality or political views, use the same techniques to get messages across in punchy and vivid ways.

The disadvantage of citing famous speakers is that it's likely to prompt a worrying question that often arises when people are first being exposed to these techniques. It's all very well, they say, to use quotations from the great and the good, but they're all gifted speakers. They're blessed with a natural ability to produce punchy lines without giving it a second thought, whereas I'm not gifted and therefore won't be able to get my own messages across with anything like the same impact.

In fact, nothing could be further from the truth. Once you are familiar with the techniques used by naturally gifted communicators, anyone can learn to use them for themselves, whether you're making a business presentation (Step 5) or a speech at a wedding or other social occasion (Step 6).

Step 4 Summary
Inspiring Your Audience

1. **Contrasts:**
   - Contradictions: 'not this but that'
   - Comparisons: 'more this than that'
   - Opposites: 'black or white'
   - Phrase reversals

2. **Puzzles and questions:**
   - Puzzle-solution format
   - Rhetorical questions

3. **Lists of three:**
   - Three identical words
   - Three different words
   - Three phrases
   - Three clauses
   - Three sentences

4. **Combinations:**
Any of the first three techniques can be combined in various ways that are likely to have an even greater impact than any single one used on its own.

5. **Painting pictures with words:**
   - Similes
   - Metaphors
   - Analogies
   - Anecdotes
   - The sound of words: alliteration

Step 5

Presenting to Business Audiences

In courses on business presentation skills, I make extensive use of video clips from political speeches to illustrate the techniques that make for effective speaking. One of the advantages of this is that politicians are professional communicators. As some of them are widely recognised as better communicators than average, we can learn from observing how they do it. But a disadvantage is that it sometimes prompts doubt in the minds of people whose main speaking commitment is the business presentation. After all, they point out, political messages are very different from business messages: they are much more emotive, and, unlike political speeches, management presentations are more concerned with cool analysis and the communication of facts and information. So just how appropriate is it to use the same techniques to get business messages across?

Those who raise these issues hardly ever realise that, in making these points, they have already made rather effective use of a contrast – the perceived differences between political messages on the one hand, and business messages on the other. They also underestimate just how many business presentations are concerned with persuading an audience, whether it is about the benefits of a product, a proposal, a change in strategy, or simply that the speaker is doing an excellent job for the company.

However, regardless of the particular objectives, the important point is that these techniques can work at different levels. Certainly they are very effective for packaging emotive messages that are intended to inspire and sway an audience. But they are just as useful for breaking down complex material into the kinds of short, digestible chunks that audiences find easy to follow. They therefore help to overcome two of the biggest problems that audiences face. First, by enabling you to say things simply, they reduce the chances of overloading audiences with too much complex information. And second, by packaging messages in ways that are known to go down well with audiences, you're more likely to hold their attention and interest, and may even enthuse and inspire them.

Armed with the knowledge that *how* a message is packaged can make a world of difference to an audience, and with the Step 4 toolkit, anyone can start to compose punchy lines for themselves. I know this because I've seen people doing it on hundreds of courses, and what impresses me most is just how quickly they learn to do it. In fact, I have never run a course on presentation and public speaking that lasted for more than two days, and many have been shorter than that. To underline the point, the extracts in this section are all real examples that were produced by course participants who had been exposed to the techniques described earlier for no more than one day.

Contrasts

In this first example, the original version of the message was formulated in the kind of written formal-sounding language that was typical within the company in question:

> In this presentation I'm going to talk to you about the need to set objectives and formulate an action plan in response to significant anticipated growth in the number of new products announced by International Digital Technology from 497 in the last full year to a tentatively projected figure of a thousand per annum three years hence.

In translating this into a punchier form, the speaker singled out the key point about the dramatic increase in the number of new products, and used the simple contrast as an example of a pre-introduction (*see Step 2*):

> [A] In 2006, IDT launched around 500 new products.
>
> [B] By 2010, this number will have increased to a staggering one thousand new products during the year.
>
> *(Name of company, numbers and dates changed to protect anonymity)*

When it comes to highlighting dramatic changes over time, a simple contrast between two dates and two facts is an extremely simple and economical way of getting the point across. Rather than spoon-feeding the audience with lots of irrelevant data that they are unlikely to remember, it allows them to draw their own conclusion. The following is an almost identical example from a talk by a famous management guru:

> [A] In 1970 it took 108 guys five days to unload
>   a timber ship.
> [B] That same activity today takes eight people
>   one day.
>
> **Tom Peters**

The next example came right at the end of a presentation in which the speaker wanted to leave his audience with the following basic message:

> The various points I have outlined in this
> presentation point to the need for us to do even
> better in the future.

He chose to reformulate this using a comparative contrast ('more this than that'), and 'today' and 'tomorrow' as metaphors for the present and future:

> So the important thing
> [A] is not how good we are today,
> [B] but how much better we need to be tomorrow.

As with many of the other examples in this book, there is great scope here for changing a word or two to get across whatever particular message you want to convey. In this case, for instance, the line would work just as well if it included various other comparisons, as in these variations on the same theme:

> [A]... not how profitable we are today,
> but how much more profitable we need to be
> tomorrow.
>
> [B]... not how successful we are today,
> but how much more successful we need to be
> tomorrow.

The following rather neutral-sounding statement does little to dramatise the pressing importance of the situation:

> In order to continue in business, the company is
> being forced to rationalise various aspects of its
> organisation.

By translating it into a contradictory contrast ('not this but that'), the speaker was able to convey a greater sense of urgency:

> [A] Rationalisation is not an option.
> [B] It's an absolute necessity for survival.

Puzzles And Questions

Moving Smoothly Between Sections of a Presentation

Most speakers find that the easiest technique to master is the puzzle-solution format, and the posing of rhetorical questions. As mentioned earlier, questions are particularly useful for pointing the way forward to the next section of a presentation. This not only gets the audience to start thinking about what's coming next, but also relieves them of having to listen to repetitive and overworked lines like those in italics in the left-hand column below. The alternatives on the right use questions to do the same job.

Moving on now to our strengths...	If those are our weaknesses, what are our strengths?
The next slide shows a list of steps involved in preparing for the strategic review.	So what steps are we taking to prepare for the strategic review?

In the first of these examples, the word 'strengths' in the question contrasts with the 'weaknesses' in the previous clause. As the following examples show, this is quite a common feature of this type of bridge between two sections of a presentation. Contrasts are made between last year and next year, the UK and Europe and problems and solutions:

> I've taken you through the figures for last year, but what are our plans for the next one?
>
> That's what our business looks like in the UK, but how is it shaping up in the rest of Europe?
>
> I've outlined the problems, but what about the solutions?

Attracting Attention in the First Place

The examples so far have involved using questions to get the audience interested at the start of a new section. In the same way, puzzles and questions can be used as pre-introductions (*see Step* 2) at the beginning of a presentation to engage the attention of the audience. For example, the speaker in the following example had to introduce some of his colleagues to a campaign aimed at increasing customer awareness of the high quality of their company's goods and services. He decided that the best way to get into the subject was by starting with a puzzle:

> I'd like to start by posing a question.
>
> **PUZZLE**   Is there any point in being good at something if people don't know you're good at it?
>
> **SOLUTION**   The obvious answer, in business at least, is no…

From an audience point of view, a riddle of this kind is obviously much more likely to attract their interest and attention than having to listen for a hundredth time to a list of agenda items prefaced by the commonest opening line of all: 'In this presentation I'm going to talk about…'

I was once asked to coach the finance director of a multinational company for a presentation at an annual management conference. In previous years, he had received very poor ratings from delegates. This was because he had rambled incomprehensibly through slides containing nothing but tables of numbers so small that he was the only one near enough to read them. Having persuaded him of the importance of getting off to a good start, he tried to find the word 'finance' in the index of various dictionaries of quotations. Interestingly, it was nowhere to be found in any of them. So he looked up 'money' instead, and came up with a puzzling simile from Somerset Maugham:

> PUZZLE Money is like a sixth sense.
> SOLUTION Without it you can't make full use
> of the other five.

He then changed 'money' to 'finance', and used it as the opening line of his presentation, following it up with three metaphors, and a contrast outlining the overall structure of what was to come:

> In our business finance has other roles as well.
> [1] It's a map for seeing where we are,
> [2] a compass for putting us in the right
> direction,
> [3] and the fuel for getting us to our destination.
> So I want this morning to take a look at
> [A] where we are today
> [B] and where we're going tomorrow.

Many of those who had suffered his presentation at the previous year's conference said that, as soon as they heard this opening sequence, their fears evaporated. Some even went as far as to rate it as 'a hundred times better' than his earlier incoherent ramblings. Even the less exaggerated evaluations were unanimous in giving him much higher ratings than he'd ever had before.

Three-Part Lists

As the last example shows, lists of three can also be used effectively in business presentations. They are second only to rhetorical questions in terms of the ease with which people are able to start producing creative lines of their own. They quickly discover that it's possible to condense all kinds of different subjects into three headings, often managing to put the longest item in third position:

> The strategy has three main purposes:
> to boost the industry's confidence,
> to enhance the credibility of the council
> and to open the way for new initiatives in
> consumer promotions.

They learn that audiences will assume that there are three things coming up, whether or not this is announced in advance, and that it certainly isn't necessary to introduce each point with 'firstly', 'secondly' and 'thirdly'.

> Our company enjoys a high reputation on a
> number of fronts:
> the quality of our products and services,
> our contribution to the UK economy
> and our determination to succeed in a rapidly
> changing business environment.

People also discover that various forms of repetition they would never dream of using when writing a letter or proposal actually sound quite natural when spoken aloud. This can be seen in the following examples from presentations by different speakers:

> To be a truly global player, you need a truly
> global service provider,
> with *the right* expertise,
> *the right* knowledge
> and *the right* understanding to meet your needs.
>
> Customers *will gain*, the company *will gain* and
> staff *will gain*.
>
> They are *out of* touch, *out of* date and *out of* work.

Combined Formats

Some years ago, I worked with a director of an electricity supply company. He was preparing for a public meeting at which he was going to have to speak on the rather delicate issue of his company's policy on disconnecting customers who were either unable or unwilling to pay their bills. He was very aware that the attitude of many in the audience would be along the lines of 'it's all very well for you, but you don't know what it's like to be so poor that you can't pay for the basic necessities of life'. He decided to address the issue head-on by starting his speech on a personal note. This aimed to show that he did understand the problems faced by low-income families and individuals. The sequence began with a contrast between two lists of three:

> Like many of you here tonight,
> [A] I have a job, a good standard of living, and no problems in paying my utilities bill.
> [B] But some of our customers have no job, a low standard of living and very real problems paying their bills.

The scope for combining different techniques to get points across in business presentations is no less than in political speeches. The following different types of combination are further examples produced by speakers within a few hours of having first heard about the basic principles.

Contrast Followed by Three-part List

[A] We've got to move from informing people
[B] to involving people.
[1] And that means clear priorities,
[2] clear targets
[3] and clear measures of performance.

Contrast, the Second Part of which is a Three-part List

[A] We'll succeed not by luck,
[B] [1, 2, 3] but by listening, talking and responding to customers.

Puzzle Solved by Two Contrasting Similes and a Three-part List

PUZZLE   How do we compare in the great scheme of things?
SOLUTION   [A] We're like a David
            [B] to Microsoft's Goliath,
            [A] a TVR
            [B] to General Motors.
            [1, 2, 3] Small in size, big on quality and successful niche players in the global marketplace.

Imagery And Anecdotes

As is clear from some of these examples, there is no problem in using metaphors and similes in business presentations. Anecdotes, too, can be used as illustrative examples to get key points across in a vivid and memorable way, a point that has been underlined by business gurus such as Tom Peters, Rosabeth Moss Kanter and Gary Hamel. All of them make extensive use of carefully selected stories, many of which are designed to prompt laughter from the audience.

One case that clearly demonstrated how effective anecdotes can be in getting key messages across occurred at a conference on crisis management. The speaker who got the highest audience ratings by far was the only one who didn't use slides with long lists of *do's* and *don'ts*. Instead, he told two contrasting anecdotes to illustrate alternative ways in which an organisation can approach its dealings with the media. In one case, a refusal to release information to the press resulted in reporters trying to find out what had happened from neighbours and others outside the organisation. As a result, the coverage relied heavily on rumour and gossip, and reflected badly on the organisation in question. In the second case, a more open and cooperative approach resulted in media coverage that took the side of the organisation in crisis, and had a positive impact on its public image.

Liberating Speakers To Be Themselves

The aim of this chapter has been to demonstrate that the techniques described earlier can be quickly grasped and put to work by political speakers and business presenters. Perhaps most encouraging of all is the fact that, once equipped with the necessary toolkit, beginners discover creative abilities within themselves of which they hadn't previously been aware. They also find that planning presentations becomes less of a chore to be dreaded, and can even be quite enjoyable.

They regularly report that they feel liberated, and that much more of their personality comes across than when they were trying to conform to the industry-standard model of presentation. And at the heart of the transformation is the experience of achieving better rapport than ever before with audiences that show no signs at all of falling asleep.

Step 5 Summary
Presenting to Business Audiences

Getting your messages across effectively isn't just a matter of deciding what you want to say, but should also involve working out *how* to say it in a way that's likely to have a positive impact on the audience. To do this, use techniques from the timeless toolkit in Step 4:

- Contrast
- Puzzles and questions
- Three-part lists
- Combined format
- Imagery and anecdotes

Step 6

Making Wedding and Social Speeches

I once went to a wedding at which the groom made the following speech:

> I'd just like to thank everyone for coming. And thanks also to [the bride's] mum and dad for arranging everything, and to my mum and dad for all their help and support. So if you'd just raise your glasses I'd like to propose a toast to the bridesmaids.

After proposing the toast, he sat down and handed over to the best man, who had flown in from abroad especially for the occasion. His speech, also reproduced here in full, went as follows:

> I'd just like to say thank you on behalf of the bridesmaids. And, er, I've got some cards here to read out... [*reads out greetings cards*]

The speech ended when he finished reading out the last word on the last card. To say that the audience felt a sense of anticlimax would be a serious understatement. On such occasions, they expect a little bit more than this, even allowing for the fact that the key players may have little or no experience of speech-making.

Weddings, of course, are only one of a wide range of social occasions at which almost anyone might find themselves having to speak. This might be to propose a vote of thanks, to present a retirement gift to a departing colleague or to introduce an after-dinner speaker. If you are the groom, the best man or the father of the bride at a wedding, you have no choice but to stand up and say at least a few words. Tens of thousands of such speeches are taking place every week, and they probably provoke more fear and dread than any other type of speech-making. A major reason for this is that, in a very high proportion of cases, it is the first speech the speaker has ever had to make.

Reasons For Reassurance

This chapter looks at how the techniques described so far can help ease the pain of being called upon to make a social or duty speech. The first and most important thing to be said is that all the basic principles covered in this book can be used just as effectively on these social occasions as at political rallies or business presentations. And there are some added bonuses for social and duty speakers that are quite reassuring and help boost confidence in the face of so daunting a task.

In the first place, the challenge of keeping the audience awake is much less of a problem than in many other situations. This is for three main reasons:

1. These are speeches that audiences positively look forward to as the focal point of an occasion. Everyone can concentrate for a few moments on the reason why they are all there. You can therefore take heart from the fact that you are doing something everyone expects and wants to be done, but no one actually wants to do.

2. Social speeches are, or should be, fairly short. Ideally, they should last only a few minutes rather than a few tens of minutes.

3. You don't have to worry about how to simplify complex material into a form that audiences

will be able to understand. The subject matter is much more straightforward and clearly defined, as the central topic of the vast majority of social and duty speeches is one particular person or, in the case of weddings, two people.

In Praise Of People

When it comes to speaking about particular individuals, the techniques described earlier are just as adaptable for packaging messages about a person as they are for talking about any other subject. For example, the opening lines of the most famous funeral oration in English literature included a three-part list and two consecutive contrasts:

> Friends, Romans and Countrymen.
> Lend me your ears.
> I come to bury Caesar, not to praise him.
> The evil that men do lives after them;
> the good is oft interred with their bones.
> So let it be with Caesar.
>
> **Shakespeare (*Julius Caesar*)**

And, as we saw earlier, Lord Spencer began his speech at the funeral of his sister, Diana, Princess of Wales, with a three-part list:

> I stand before you today the representative of a family in grief, in a country in mourning before a world in shock.
>
> **Lord Spencer**

Ronald Reagan's address after the Challenger shuttle disaster in 1986 featured a puzzle about why there was a coincidence that day. He solved this by comparing the astronauts with a famous explorer of the past, inserting a three-part quotation along the way:

> There's a coincidence today.
> On this day 390 years ago, the great explorer Sir Francis Drake died aboard ship off the coast of Panama. In his lifetime the great frontiers were the oceans, and a historian later said, 'He lived by the sea, died on it, and was buried in it.' Well, today, we can say of the Challenger crew: Their dedication was, like Drake's, complete.
>
> **Ronald Reagan**

Although these examples come from the public domain, a central message of this book is that exactly the same techniques that work so well for the famous can be used just as easily and effectively by anyone else. As in the earlier discussion of business presentations, none of the following examples is invented and all are taken from real speeches made at various types of social occasion.

Three Virtues

Whether the speech is a funeral address, or any other type of speech about a particular person, it is very easy to divide points up into lists of three:

> As a child, he was cheeky, naughty and the loudest kid in school.
>
> As far as he was concerned, obstacles were merely there to be overcome.
> Red tape was there to be cut through.
> And visions were there to be turned into reality.
>
> He is one of the friendliest, funniest and most generous people I've ever met.

Inserting a third item that contrasts with the first two introduces an element of surprise and humour into the sequence, as in the following comments by the best man at a wedding:

> He was well known throughout the college for his companionship, good humour and unswerving faith in the fortunes of Oxford United.

The same three-part format can be used to deliver the solution to a puzzle. The unexpected third item prompts laughter:

> When it came to his job, he had three unstoppable qualities:
> professionalism, determination and downright obstinacy.

Contrasting Qualities

Contrasts are also useful for summing up a person's essential qualities:

> In her life she taught me the meaning of friendship.
> Her death has taught me the meaning of courage.

At a dinner for the old boys of an all-male school, one of the speakers proposed a toast to the girls from the local school for girls – with whom many of those present had had their first dates. A woman guest who had been at the girls' school in question replied on their behalf with a single sentence consisting of a contrast that rearranged the words in the first part. It went down so well with the audience that they responded with a spontaneous standing ovation:

> The girls you all remember [PAUSE] all remember you.

Imagery

The various kinds of imagery discussed earlier are often used to highlight a feature of someone's character:

> For him, new technology was always a servant, never the master.
>
> He was like a corporate gardener, sowing seeds today so that the company could reap the harvest tomorrow.

Anecdotes

Of all the techniques described earlier, the one that really comes into its own in social and duty speeches is the anecdote. A well-chosen story that represents some key characteristic of a person can be so effective that it is often the only thing that anyone ever remembers about such speeches. Sometimes, anecdotes are as short as a single sentence, as in the following example, which was introduced to illustrate what the speaker meant by describing the person in question as 'a great romantic'.

> When I was ill in hospital, he managed to smuggle in smoked salmon and a bottle of wine, physical tokens of the love and support that helped me through, and speeded my recovery.

More usually, anecdotes extend over several sentences, as at the funeral of a man in his 20s who had died suddenly from an undiagnosed heart condition. The centrepiece of the eulogy by one of his friends was widely commended afterwards by the mourners as a brilliant summing-up of the essence of his character. The story was set at a beach bar in the Far East:

Having partied the night away, the rest of us were faltering. But Johnny was determined to squeeze the last drop of fun from his holiday. As we sloped off, Johnny, as only he could do, managed to get chatting to two Canadian circus performers and an Irish girl, who instantly took a shine to him. As they got chatting, a rather large man at the bar took umbrage to it, as he was under the impression he was with the girl. He proceeded to charge at Johnny in a drunken attempt to attack him. However, on his way, he stumbled in the sand and fell at Johnny's feet. But Johnny was completely oblivious and, thinking he had fallen over, helped him up, dusted him off and asked if he was all right – to which his assailant replied with a head butt. Johnny, definitely a lover not a fighter, turned tail and made a run for it – at which point his new circus performer pals saw his predicament and chased his attacker into the sea... Although funny, the story also shows to me Johnny's natural temptation to see the good in people. In every way, he was a predominantly good person, and it was one of the things I now realise I admired and also relied on the most.

It struck a chord with the congregation because it highlighted characteristics that everyone could recognise as typical of the deceased. And what made it all the more impressive was the fact that it was the first speech that the speaker had ever made in his life.

Lines For Any Occasion

An interesting feature of these examples is that, although they may originally have been used at weddings, funerals or parties to celebrate a birthday or the achievements of a departing colleague, most of them could have been used on any occasion where the focus of the speech was on a particular person. Even in the case of the anecdote from the young man's funeral, it's easy to imagine the same story being told (apart from the last sentence) at his wedding, or at a party celebrating his promotion or move from one job to another. This demonstrates the general applicability of the techniques and approach described in this book, and the fact that the preparation and delivery of social and duty speeches is much the same as that of preparing and delivering any other kind of speech.

The main difference between the various types of social speech lies in mood, emphasis and striking a suitable balance between humour and seriousness. At the two extremes are funeral addresses and the best man's speech at weddings. But a eulogy that is completely serious is unlikely to be as effective as one that includes some humorous lines or anecdotes about the deceased. These are not only an effective way of recalling affectionate memories about someone's life and character, but can also help to relieve some of the sadness that permeates the atmosphere at funerals and memorial services. At the other extreme, the balance shifts towards more humour than seriousness in the best man's speech at weddings. However, as will be seen later, this is not without its dangers, and doesn't mean that a best man's speech should be entirely lacking in serious content.

Analysing The Audience

When preparing a wedding or social speech, knowledge of who is going to be in the audience is so critical that it's worth doing some research beforehand. At family occasions such as weddings and funerals, there are likely to be people from widely differing age groups; there may be a complicated collection of ex-spouses and stepchildren to take into account; or there may be people of different nationalities, religions or ethnic backgrounds.

In speeches marking a colleague's retirement, you need to be aware of any special tensions there may have been between the person who is leaving and others who might be present, as well as any other office politics that might complicate matters. Knowing about the audience mix not only helps to minimise the chances of giving needless offence, but can also guide you towards the most suitable ways of wording particular sections of a speech. And the safest way to avoid giving offence to some or all of those present is to steer clear of any humour that might come across as sexist, racist or blue. Sexual innuendo and smutty jokes may go down well enough with some audiences that are young and male, but are unlikely to win many friends at family gatherings that include all age groups from the very young to the very old.

The Search For Stories

Anecdotes play such an important part in wedding and social speeches that, whatever the occasion, a major part of the preparation process should involve a search for suitable stories. These should be both serious and humorous, and illustrate some essential feature of the person's character, work or lifestyle. By far the best place to start is by asking other people who know or knew the individual concerned. This is because their response to such a request will invariably go beyond merely producing a list of descriptive adjectives ('kind', 'loyal', 'witty', 'generous' and so on) to give examples that back up these descriptions. Such examples tend to consist of stories that illustrate the particular characteristics mentioned.

Consulting with others is not only important as a means of gathering raw material, but also has another important advantage. Those who make social and duty speeches are rarely expected to confine themselves to their personal feelings, but have a wider responsibility to represent and speak on behalf of everyone else. If we are members of the person's family, there may be details of their work or leisure pursuits that we know nothing about, while work colleagues may be just as ignorant of their family life. But one of the reassuring things about the search for stories that sum up a person's character is that they typically reveal a high level of agreement about what the person in question is really like. The stories we collect will therefore almost invariably reflect and confirm our own views, and give us the confidence to develop them when preparing the speech.

Avoiding Overlap
As there tends to be a convergence of opinion about any particular individual, the first question to be asked by anyone invited to speak about someone is whether or not there will be any other speakers. If there are, it's extremely important to have a word

with them in advance about what points they are planning to make, and which anecdotes they will be using by way of illustration. Otherwise, there's always a risk of overlap and repetitiveness. On one occasion, for example, a speaker at a funeral told me how relieved he had been to have spoken first, as all those who followed him did little more than go over the themes he'd already mentioned.

Wedding Speeches

Traditionally, three main categories of people – the bride's father (or close relation or family friend), the groom and the best man – speak at a wedding. For the first two, there is a fairly standard blueprint that makes it reasonably straightforward to decide what to say. Bridegrooms and fathers of the bride can also draw comfort from the fact that members of the audience are perfectly well aware that weddings are very emotional occasions for the main participants and their parents, and don't really expect either of these first two speeches to be the entertaining high spot of the proceedings. By contrast, the best man is in the unenviable position of being expected to go beyond his official duty of responding on behalf of the bridesmaids and reading out greetings cards, to supply the entertainment and release from formality that everyone has been waiting for. As such, it is perhaps the most challenging social speech that anyone is ever likely to have to make.

Minimally, the points to be dealt with by the father of the bride are as follows:

- Thank people for coming.
- Refer to friends and relations who could not be present.
- Tell stories about his daughter's life so far.
- Welcome the groom into the family.
- Propose a toast to the bride and groom.

Replying to the toast is the main job of the groom's speech, which is likely to include some or all of the following:

- Thank the bride's parents, his parents, everyone else involved in organising and helping at the wedding, the guests for coming and for the wedding presents.
- Present gifts to bridesmaids, pageboys, ushers and so on.
- Comment on how the day is going so far.
- Story of how the romance developed.
- Express delight at having married his bride.
- Compliment, thank and then propose a toast to the bridesmaids.

A sure-fire way for the groom to get cheers and applause from the audience is the simple phrase 'my wife and I', which can be exploited by repeating it at various points during the speech.

The Best Man's Speech

I have already stressed the importance of speakers avoiding forms of language and styles of delivery that make them sound as if they are trying to play the part of someone else. Many a best man, anxious about his audience's expectations, tries to play a part that doesn't come naturally to him. As a result, many speeches consist of an endless succession of jokes and supposedly funny stories about the groom – often poorly delivered, and usually giving the impression that the groom is an idle layabout and serial sex maniac, whose main interest in life is getting drunk.

This trend is actively encouraged by the hundreds of best man speeches found on the internet, many of which use the same jokes, and assume that the main objective is to humiliate the groom. This may amuse a minority of those present – the groom's friends perhaps – but reflects an insensitive analysis of the wider audience as a whole. Many are likely to find such material at best inappropriate, and at worst downright embarrassing or offensive. This is not to say that all humour directed towards the groom should be eliminated, but there is a world of difference between outright character assassination and poking gentle fun at someone. There is also much to be said for softening the mockery of his foibles and eccentricities by contrasting these with some of his positive assets.

A nice example of this was directed at a groom who was widely known to have excelled academically at school and university, and who could therefore hardly be made out to be a shiftless good-for-nothing. The best man read out extracts from early school reports that highlighted the contrast between the glowing comments about his academic performance and his complete hopelessness in practical subjects like woodwork. He then rounded the sequence off by noting that this explained the absence of DIY equipment on the wedding present list, and warned the bride not to expect him to be much use as a handyman around the house.

Apart from school reports, various other sources of material can sometimes provide themes that you can develop in a light-hearted way. There may be a topical event in the news that relates in some way to the groom's job, hobbies or interests. Dictionaries of dates occasionally reveal that some famous occurrence happened on the day the groom was born, and provide a basis for amusing comparisons to be made. It is also worth remembering that many first names originally had a meaning that might reflect or be at odds with the known characteristics of the groom. The astrological star signs of the bride and groom can also sometimes be mined for humorous purposes, as too can the predictions of newspaper horoscopes published on the wedding day itself (even if these are actually your own inventions).

Although the best man's speech will include a greater proportion of humorous material than most other types of social and duty speech, there is still a need for a certain amount of serious content. Even the minimalist example at the beginning of this chapter managed to include thanks for the toast to the bridesmaids and the reading out of cards. The more serious aspects of the best man's job will normally include some or all of the following:

- Thanks on behalf of the bridesmaids for the groom's toast to them.
- Reading out the cards from people unable to attend the wedding.
- Comments on the attractiveness of the bride and bridesmaids, on the wedding ceremony itself and the atmosphere of the proceedings so far.

- As the best man is the only one in the wedding line-up whose role includes speaking on behalf of all the guests, he may also wish to propose a collective vote of thanks to the parents of the bride and groom and everyone else involved in providing the hospitality.
- Act as master of ceremonies (if there is no official one), including:
  - bringing the gathering to order;
  - introducing the other speakers;
  - making any announcements that may be necessary.

Using Names To Prompt Applause

Whether introducing a guest, proposing a vote of thanks, commending or congratulating someone or awarding a prize or a gift to a colleague who is leaving or retiring, the speaker will want at some stage to set things up so that the audience shows their collective approval for the person in question. A common formula for doing this is the overworked cliché: 'Let us all now show our appreciation in the usual manner.' Effective enough though this may be, it is such a blunt and direct instruction that it's rather like using a sledgehammer to bludgeon the audience into applauding on demand. A rather more subtle and indirect way of orchestrating applause is to exploit the fact that audiences are very used to the idea of applauding when they hear someone's name – provided it occurs right at the end of a sequence.

For a naming to work smoothly, the name has to come last in a sequence involving four distinct phases:

1. Identify the person being introduced/thanked/congratulated.
2. Say something about them.
3. PAUSE
4. Name them.

A typical example of this is as follows:

1. Our next speaker is our marketing director
2. who's done such a great job since joining us two years ago:
3. PAUSE
4. Alan Adman. [Applause]

The first stage informs the audience that the speaker is about to introduce someone and who that person is. The second says something about his virtues. The pause between that and the name gives them time to get ready to applaud, so that they are poised to start as soon as, or – as often happens – just before the speaker finishes saying the name.

This basic formula can be adapted in various ways to meet the particular needs of an occasion. For example, when introducing speakers or giving a vote of thanks, you can extend the second stage to include more details about the person in question. In other situations, such as when reading out the nominations for prizes before naming the winners, you may want to keep the audience guessing about the identity of the person right up to the last second. The identity of the person to be named tends to be withheld in exactly the same way when hosts of television talk shows introduce their guests. To create such an air of suspense, all you have to do is to leave out the first step in the sequence and use stage 2 to give clues as to their identity:

1. My next guest is someone who made his name as the Saint, became even better known as James Bond and is now heavily involved as a roving ambassador for UNICEF:
2. PAUSE
3. Ladies and gentlemen, Roger Moore. [Applause]

When using this technique, things can go badly wrong if you don't get each stage in the right order.

I once saw this happen at a college meeting when the principal spent part of his speech thanking various people with lines like 'I'd like to thank Joe Bloggs and his team of gardeners for creating such an attractive backdrop to our daily life and work'. After a second or two of silence, one or two isolated claps were followed by what could only be described as a hesitant round of applause. The same thing happened several times in a row as the speaker thanked various other people for their contribution to the life of the college. Afterwards, members of the audience were to be heard complaining that they had found it all rather embarrassing because they'd been unsure exactly when to applaud – a problem that would certainly not have arisen if the speaker had followed the simple formula described above.

Mastering The Ceremonies

The technique of orchestrating things so that an audience starts to applaud at the mention of a name is a useful part of the toolkit for anyone who has to take the chair, or act as the master of ceremonies, at functions where social speeches play a part. And having someone in charge of making sure that everything runs smoothly is a key part in the organisation of such events. The importance of the role is underlined by the fact that, for very formal occasions, professional toastmasters or masters of ceremonies are often employed to preside over the proceedings. But in the vast majority of situations, the role of MC falls to an amateur, such as the best man at a wedding.

Whether professional or amateur, the MC's first job is to find out who will be speaking, and the order in which the speeches will take place. This includes not only being sure about what their names are, but also about the names by which they prefer to be known. There may, for example, be a question about whether to use titles, and, if so, whether to refer to people as 'Mr', 'Mrs', 'Ms', 'Dr', 'Professor' and so on. It's also as well to know which form of name to use: 'William Shakespeare', 'Will', 'Bill' or 'Billy'. Otherwise, embarrassing situations can arise, such as the wedding of a man who had always been called by his second Christian name. This crucial piece of information had apparently not reached the vicar, who, much to everyone's surprise (groom and bride included), referred to him throughout the service by his first name.

At some stage, the MC will have to decide exactly when to start the formal proceedings. This usually means checking with the speakers that they're ready to start, or having a word with the caterers to keep the clattering of crockery to a minimum. Where people are eating, or milling about with drinks in their hands, your next problem is how to quell the noise so that everyone can concentrate on the speeches. This calls for decisiveness on the part of an MC. And doing something invariably works better than trying to say something, as it will be difficult for anyone to hear your voice above the general hubbub created by all the other voices. In the absence of a gavel or a gong, the best plan is to stand up and bang a spoon on the table or against a glass – and to keep it up until the noise shows signs of subsiding. Even then, there's no guarantee of instant success, and initial attempts to impose silence on an audience, especially when people are in high spirits, often fail. Your challenge is to put a stop to all the conversations that are taking place at the same time, which may mean banging your spoon for quite some time before the audience settles down enough for everyone to be able to hear and listen to what you have to say.

Introductions

As the MC's main responsibility is to orchestrate the smooth running of the proceedings, you don't have to speak for very long, or to do anything else that might divert the limelight away from the main speaker(s). You're unlikely to have to do more than welcome the guests and thank them for coming, before going on to introduce the speaker(s). As we saw earlier, this is one of the places where getting the audience to applaud at the mention of a name really comes into its own. The only preparation the MC has to do is to decide what and how much to say about the person who is about to speak (stage 2 in the technique), as a preamble to pausing (stage 3) and naming them (stage 4). At weddings, this is very straightforward, as the main players all occupy the familiar standardised roles of bride, groom, best man and so on. This means that there is no need for you to say anything more than, 'Our first speaker is the bride's father: [pause] Mr Albert Smith.'

In other situations, such as introductions to a guest speaker or visiting lecturer, it is usual to provide rather more background information. It may, for example, be appropriate to say something about the speaker's job, interests, qualifications or achievements, and to mention the reason why they have been invited to speak to this particular audience on this particular occasion. However, in reaching a decision, the main point to remember is that the audience is there to listen to the visiting speaker, not to the MC, which means that brevity is your safest route to a successful introduction.

Off The Cuff

There are some situations, such as public meetings or at the end of a lecture, when we find ourselves with an opportunity to speak, or may be called upon to say something without any prior warning. These are occasions about which Mark Twain had some rather worrying advice when he said, 'It usually takes me three weeks to prepare a good impromptu speech.' The serious point here is that you will usually have some idea in advance that you might have to speak, which means that it's well worth making the effort to have some lines ready just in case.

On the fairly rare occasions when there is no advance warning whatsoever, the most important thing is to have been listening to the proceedings before the dreaded moment when you're called upon to speak. This gives you a fair chance of rising to the occasion and saying something that actually relates to what has gone before. And, if you can think of three things, produce a suitable contrast or come up with a relevant anecdote, the chances are that you'll have succeeded beyond most people's expectations. In other words, much the same criteria apply as for any other speech, the main difference being the need for some extremely quick thinking.

Using A Microphone

Speakers at social occasions often find themselves having to use a microphone for the first time in their lives. If you're unprepared for it, this can add to the stress of the situation.

Don't be Surprised by the Sound of Your Voice Echoing Back at You

Most people aren't used to hearing the sound of their voice being amplified around a room, and often find the experience quite unnerving. On the plus side, however, the echoing effect tends to help speakers to slow down, pause more and therefore deliver the speech at a more appropriate pace.

Try to Avoid Using a Hand-held Microphone

Although holding a microphone up to the mouth may work perfectly well for professional singers, it can be a nightmare when making a speech, especially if you're using notes or a script. It's not just that it's quite difficult to juggle cards or paper in one hand and a microphone in the other, but the really serious fumbling sets in when you try to turn over a page. If you have to keep putting the mike down on the table, it will not only put you off, but will also be an unwelcome distraction for the audience as the thud of putting it down or the sound of rustling of paper is amplified for all to hear. Much better is to make sure that the microphone is on a stand that can be adjusted to your height – and don't forget that moving towards and away from it can cause your voice to keep fading in and fading out.

Better still is the type of microphone that clips onto your clothes and lets you forget about it altogether. These usually have a radio transmitter that can be hidden in a pocket, liberating you from being glued to one spot and allowing you to move around if you feel like it.

Most venues that host weddings, parties, conferences and so on will have such equipment available. A telephone call is usually all that's needed to make sure you won't have to use a hand-held microphone. In the rare instances where there is no choice, get someone to hold it for you so that your hands are free to manage your notes with a minimum of stress.

Don't Get Too Close to the Microphone

The commonest mistake made by people who are inexperienced at using a microphone is to put their mouths too close to it, which usually makes sound distorted and/or far too loud. If at all possible, it's well worth getting to the venue before the event starts to check voice levels and find out the best distance between mouth and microphone.

Conclusion

Wedding and social speeches are a major source of anxiety because so many people who have to give them have little or no experience of public speaking. If you are one of these, you can rely on the basic principles outlined in the rest of this book to see you through. And, as was mentioned at the start of this chapter, you have some important advantages that are not always enjoyed by other speakers, lecturers or presenters. The subject matter is typically simple and straightforward, so you aren't faced with the problem of having to simplify detailed or complex material, and you're hardly ever expected to speak for more than a few minutes to an audience that is usually in a very receptive mood.

Step 6 Summary
Making Wedding and Social Speeches

1. **Reasons for reassurance:**
   - The audience is likely to be grateful that you are doing something they all expect and want to be done, but no one actually wants to do.
   - You aren't expected to speak for more than a few minutes.
   - The subject matter is straightforward and clearly defined.
   - All the techniques from Step 4 work just as well in these as they do in any other type of speech.

2. **Preparation:**
   - As most speeches of this kind are directed towards particular individuals, anecdotes about them are an extremely important ingredient.
   - In analysing the audience, you should take into account age differences, the relationships between people and any delicate issues that might be involved.
   - If others are speaking on the same occasion, consult with them beforehand to make sure you don't all say the same things.

3. Master of ceremonies:

- Your main job is to ensure that everything runs as smoothly as possible.
- Your first challenge will be to quieten down the audience, which can sometimes take more time and effort than you expect.
- Find out beforehand who's going to be speaking and the order in which the speeches will take place.
- Be sure to get their names right – and use the forms by which they prefer to be known.

4. Using names to prompt applause:

- A simple and effective way of getting an audience to applaud someone is to say a few words about them, pause and then say their name.

5. Traditional sequence and roles of wedding speakers:

- Father of the bride – ends by proposing toast to the bride and groom.
- Groom – ends by proposing toast to the bridesmaids.
- Best man – responds on behalf of the bridesmaids.

Step 7

Understanding Body Language and Non-verbal Communication

In Step 1 we discussed a number of topics often grouped together under headings like 'body language' and 'non-verbal communication'. These included the role of eye contact in holding attention, and the importance of intonation, stress and pausing. Various other claims about body language are often heard. Some of these are myths and some are reality. It's important you know which is which so that you don't end up worrying unnecessarily when delivering a speech or presentation.

Myths

Is 93 Per Cent of Communication Non-verbal?

Type 'non-verbal communication', or something similar, into almost any search engine, and up will come a reference to a widely repeated report about the relative importance of verbal and non-verbal factors. The following is typical:

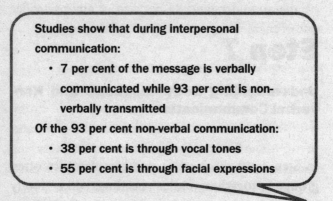

Studies show that during interpersonal communication:
- 7 per cent of the message is verbally communicated while 93 per cent is non-verbally transmitted

Of the 93 per cent non-verbal communication:
- 38 per cent is through vocal tones
- 55 per cent is through facial expressions

References to these statistics hardly ever say anything about what the research was or where it came from, but anyone who takes the trouble to look it up will discover that it simply doesn't justify such general claims.

This is hardly surprising because the reported percentages so obviously fly in the face of our common-sense experience. If true, for example, it would mean that anyone who is unable to see a speaker's facial expressions – because they are blind, in the dark, listening to a radio or talking to someone on the telephone – would only be able to understand 45 per cent of what was said to them. Most absurd of all is the fact that, if only 7 per cent is verbally communicated, there would be no need for anyone ever to learn foreign languages, as we would already be able to understand 93 per cent of any particular one of them without any formal instruction.

Are Folded Arms a Sign of Defensiveness?

Looking out on the audience in a crowded lecture theatre, I often notice that some people are sitting with their arms folded. If I believed all the modern myths about body language I would start worrying about what I'd said or done to prompt such a mass display of defensiveness. This is because it is widely claimed in the folklore of management training that people with their arms folded are on the defensive.

Luckily, I have two good reasons for not becoming too paranoid when I see people with folded arms sitting in an audience. One is that I have, on many occasions, taken the trouble to ask them if they are on the defensive. Usually, they say that they are feeling comfortable. Occasionally, they complain about the lack of armrests on the chairs, or about the inadequacies of the heating system. But never once has anyone said that they are feeling defensive. A second reason for not worrying about it is that there are invariably several people sitting with their arms folded. This is exactly what one would expect from observing how people behave in groups. It is a manifestation of our tendency to copy or reflect, albeit subconsciously, similar postures to those around us. The fact that there are a number of people with folded arms is therefore more likely to mean that they are responding to each other than mounting a collective display of defensiveness against the speaker.

If, on the other hand, we fold our arms when confronted with an awkward question or some other kind of threat, it may well be a sign of going on the defensive. This gives us a fourth possible meaning to add to comfort, missing armrests and feeling cold.

So, just like words in a language, elements of body language can have different meanings in different contexts. The trouble is that many trainers seem all too ready to accept and propagate a more rigid doctrine, in which things like folded arms are assigned a single, unambiguous and unvarying meaning in all situations. Indeed, so widely entrenched has this particular view become that I now advise that you shouldn't fold your arms when speaking, whether in a presentation, job interview or anywhere else where you're keen to make a good impression. This is not because I believe that folded arms are a sign of defensiveness, but because I know that it's very likely that there will be someone in the audience who believes that it is.

The overstated claims about the meaning of folded arms are part of a much more general trend that has gathered pace over the past two or three decades. This is the rise of various modern myths, like the 93 per cent claim discussed earlier, to the effect that body language and other non-verbal factors play an overwhelmingly important part in human communication.

Is There a Magic Formula for Dressing to Impress?

A few years ago, a delegate on one of my courses reported that, after failing to get promoted, he was told that one of the main reasons for being passed over was that he had worn a green suit at the interview. Unfortunately for him, there were members of the panel who had been informed by an image consultant to be wary of men who wear green suits to business meetings.

In effect, what consultants like this have done is identify and tap into a market that seems to be based mainly on fear and anxiety. A lot of men are so uninterested in fashion and so uncertain about what style of clothes to wear that they are prepared to pay for professional advice and reassurance. It's a market that has probably also been stimulated by an increase in the number of professional women who, unlike men, have no obvious uniform to wear at work and are therefore willing to seek an 'expert' opinion on the matter.

The point here is not that clothes don't matter at all, but that we should not be drawn into thinking that there is some scientifically based recipe that is guaranteed to enable us to convey a favourable impression to every member of every audience, regardless of the particular circumstances of the occasion. In my experience, most people get away with it through a combination of common sense and trial and error. There will obviously be times when advice and reassurance is needed, in which case family and colleagues are likely to be just as helpful as professional image consultants, and certainly a great deal cheaper.

Are Lecterns and Tables Barriers to Communication?

Whether or not audiences regard a lectern as a barrier, church architects have known for hundreds of years that it's an extremely efficient device for making it as easy as possible to read from a text. It positions a Bible with large easy-to-read print at a height and an angle that suits most adults. Readers can glance up at the congregation and down to the text without even having to move their heads, and without fear of losing their place. By comparison, tables are not such efficient resting places for notes or scripts, as they require you to glance up and down through an arc of nearly 90 degrees, which causes a more emphatic break in eye contact with the audience. But they are nonetheless extremely useful places for resting briefcases, computers, projectors and other paraphernalia associated with making a presentation.

The most sensible approach is not to avoid them altogether, but to balance their undoubted practical advantages against the possible risk of giving the audience a negative impression. For example, when speaking without notes, or from notes on cards that are stiff enough not to flap about in trembling hands, speakers have nothing to lose by deserting the lectern or table. At other times, however, the advantage of not losing one's place while retaining eye contact with the audience will almost always outweigh any disadvantages that might arise from being seen to be standing behind the lectern or table.

If you do decide to use a lectern, there's an ever-present temptation that's best avoided. Sometimes known as 'white knuckle syndrome', it occurs when you grip the sides of the lectern so tightly that the rigidity of your posture, and the nervousness that lies behind it, become visible to all. And, once you are locked into this stiff and static stance, there's almost certain to be a build-up of tension that will reduce the effectiveness of your delivery.

Do Movement and Gestures Distract?

I once worked with a trainer who taught that speakers should not only stand still, but that there was a correct stance for presentation that involved placing one foot at a particular angle slightly in front of the other. After the lecture that included this advice, members of the audience regularly came to me pointing out a glaring inconsistency between what they had just heard and what they had just seen. While recommending them not to move about when they were speaking, he had spent most of the lecture wandering about the conference room. When I asked if this worried or distracted them, they would invariably say 'no'. Most went further, adding that it helped to hold their interest and came across as lively and enthusiastic. This positive reaction to movement is in fact typical. So the best advice for the vast majority of people is that, if you feel like moving about, you should do so. Movement has the additional positive benefit of helping to disperse adrenalin and reduce tension.

The news from audiences about gestures is very similar. On almost every presentation skills course I have run, someone will say that they have been on another one where the trainer told them that gestures are distracting, and that speakers should keep their hands motionless during presentations. Yet it's as rare for audiences to give negative ratings when they see speakers gesticulating as when they see them moving about. In fact, they are much more likely to rate the use of gestures as a definite plus, often referring to it as evidence of expressiveness, individuality and liveliness.

Gestures can also be used as a form of visual aid to illustrate or emphasise a particular point. For example, when Winston Churchill spoke of an 'iron curtain' descending across Europe, he moved his left hand downwards at the same time. When Bill Clinton said that there was nothing wrong with America that couldn't be solved by what is right with America, he stabbed the air just before the words 'wrong' and 'right'. Sometimes speakers move their left hand during one part of a contrast, following it with a similar movement of the right hand during the second part. When listing three items, it's quite normal for people to count them out on their fingers, or to make three hand movements at the same time. Used in these ways, gestures look perfectly natural and play a positive part in getting the message across.

In a small minority of cases, however, speakers' movements and gestures do get a negative rating from audiences, such as when someone continually sways from side to side, takes a few steps forwards and a few steps back, over and over again, fiddles with their pen or strokes their hair. The common feature of all these bodily movements that annoy or distract audiences is their repetitiveness, which should therefore be avoided at all costs. But before being able to do that, you obviously need to know whether you are one of the minority of people who suffer from such problems. One way to find out is to ask friends and colleagues to give you some frank feedback on the issue. Another is to review a videotape of yourself in action.

Reality

Physical Tension and the Problem of Nerves

Feelings ranging from nervousness to sheer terror are common reactions for many people when faced with the prospect of having to make a speech or presentation. Being well prepared and well rehearsed takes you a long way towards defeating the problem. But this is a battle that will never be won completely, and perhaps never should be, as overconfidence almost inevitably results in a poor performance.

Speaking, whether in conversation or in front of an audience, is a much more stressful physical activity than most people realise. Quite apart from the obvious physical factors, such as breathing and moving the mouth and tongue to produce sounds recognisable as words, speaking is associated with a rise in blood pressure, irregular heartbeat and, in extreme cases, profuse sweating. But potentially the most debilitating factor is that the tension can directly affect the very parts of the body that produce the voice, causing muscles in the chest and neck to tighten. This not only restricts our ability to vary our tone and emphasis, but can also result in a quavering or more highly pitched voice than usual.

Underlying all this is the rush of adrenalin that comes from the primeval urge to fight or flee when we find ourselves in a difficult situation. Running away or assaulting the audience are obviously not serious options, which is why walking about and gesticulating help to dissipate some of the adrenalin, and why physical exercises of the kind described on page 180 can be a useful precaution to take just before making a speech.

Fear of the Audience

As well as the physical causes of tension, various psychological factors also come into play. At the heart of these is the fact that speaking to audiences is such an extremely rare event in most people's talking lives that they are not sure how to go about it, or how best to get their messages across in such an unfamiliar medium. Half the battle is therefore to understand the nature of the problem and the available solutions to it. This is why earlier steps focused on how speaking in public differs from the familiar comfortable world of everyday conversation, and on how to express ourselves in ways that will appeal to audiences.

One of the most widely cited causes of nervousness is the feeling of being threatened or exposed by being looked at by so many people all at once. This is obviously a very different experience from that of interacting with a handful of other people in a conversation, and most of us certainly feel safer sitting in an audience than standing in front of it. A commonly heard remedy is that you should imagine that members of the audience are sitting there wearing nothing but their underwear. Although this may work for some people, the trouble is that it implies that the relationship between speaker and audience is an essentially hostile one, and that you are therefore right to feel intimidated whenever you become the focus of so many people's attention. But such a view is contradicted by two important facts. Being aware of these can help to reduce the nervousness that is an almost inevitable consequence of adopting this confrontational 'us and them' attitude towards audiences.

In the first place, consider how you feel when you're sitting in the audience: do you sit there feeling hostile towards speakers, hoping to see them fall flat on their face and make a fool of themselves? If your answer is 'no', you are like the vast majority of people because – apart from very rare cases like public meetings about controversial issues – audiences are far more likely to be amicably inclined towards speakers than to be in a hostile mood of 'us *versus* them'. A second fact is that members of an audience are not, as many people seem to assume, wired up to each other in such a way as to constitute a collective mind that is somehow conspiring silently against you to bring about your downfall. A more realistic view is to think of yourself as one individual who is communicating with a number of other single individuals. Once you start viewing your relationship with the audience as consisting of a number of one-to-one encounters that happen to be taking place at the same time, it starts to feel far less intimidating.

Techniques for Tackling Tension

While movement can help to release some of the adrenalin while actually making a speech or presentation, it is also usual to experience a major build-up of tension beforehand. This can affect our voices in such a way as to cause trembling, quavering or uncertain pitch. The best way to deal with this is to tackle the main physical causes of the problem, namely tension in the neck, chest and ribcage, with a series of simple exercises aimed at freeing up and relaxing them before taking to the floor.

Most obvious, perhaps, is the fact that deep breathing and more or less any other standard relaxation exercise will help to reduce the negative effects of tension on the voice. Other simple routines are the following:

- Move the neck and head to one side as far as you can (until it starts to feel a strain to move it any further), then relax. Do the same thing in the other direction and repeat a few times.
- Move the head downwards until the chin presses against the lower neck. Relax, and then move the head backwards as far as you can. Relax again before repeating the routine a few times.
- Rotate the head in a circular motion a few times.
- Tense the shoulders upwards as far as they'll go, then relax them. Repeat a few times.
- Chew gum, or tense and relax the jaw a few times.

Breathing: The Foundation of Good Delivery

Taking deep breaths before a performance is not only good news for the calming sensation it creates. It is also essential to control the shallow breathing associated with the 'fight or flight' response brought on by feelings of nervousness.

The first step towards understanding how to breathe effectively when speaking is to learn how to control the diaphragm. This is a dome-shaped sheet of muscle located at the bottom of our lungs, which works to regulate our breathing without any conscious effort. All day and all night long it works like bellows, taking air down, and then pushing it out. But it's possible to consciously interrupt the process by pulling in enough air through our lungs to inflate the diaphragm fully. To do this, imagine there is a balloon sitting at the bottom of your lungs, and you are trying to fill it with air. Once you feel your diaphragm is inflated – you will notice your abdomen swelling outwards – release the breath slowly while speaking or humming. You will find an instant increase in the volume of sound you create, but without the hardening of sound associated with overstraining the vocal cords (which is how most people attempt to increase the sounds they make).

If Your Mouth is Not Fully Open You Will Sound Dull

An easy way to discover just how much intonation is governed by how widely we open our mouths is to try reading a speech while deliberately opening your mouth more than usual. Although it feels odd at first, opening your mouth more widely than usual goes a long way towards eliminating the problem of monotonous delivery.

So if you feel your performance is hampered by a tendency to sound monotonous, making a conscious effort to open your mouth more widely will give an instant brightening effect, and increase the tonal variation in the sounds that come out of your mouth.

Alcohol is Never the Answer

Because drinking alcohol is associated with relaxing social occasions, many people think that a drink or two will help to give them confidence before making a speech. This is one of the biggest mistakes you can ever make, for the simple reason that alcohol directly affects the brain. In excess, it causes speech to become slurred and incoherent, but even a slight amount reduces our ability to keep a clear head and will have a negative impact on performance. So the rule is simple: never drink anything alcoholic before making a speech.

However, drinking water or a soft drink before or during a presentation is a perfectly acceptable solution to the more or less inevitable problem of a dry mouth and throat.

Winning the Battle Against Tension

The final essential step towards successful speaking, then, is to minimise the negative effects of nervousness and tension. This is why you shouldn't waste time becoming needlessly anxious about some of the exaggerated myths of the supposedly overwhelming importance of body language and non-verbal behaviour. And the good news is that, as we've seen, there are some tried-and-tested techniques for combating the things that really do matter. Most people who have seen themselves in action on videotapes are pleasantly surprised to discover that they didn't come across as anything like as nervous as they felt at the time – which suggests that our inner worries are much less evident to others than we think.

Step 7 Summary
Understanding Body Language and
Non-verbal Communication

1. Claims to be sceptical about:
   - What we actually say plays a minor role in communication.
   - 93 per cent of communication is non-verbal.
   - There is a scientifically based formula for the clothes that will have most impact.
   - People with folded arms are always on the defensive.
   - Lecterns and tables are barriers to effective communication.
   - Moving about while speaking distracts the audience.
   - Using gestures distracts the audience.

2. Claims to be taken seriously:
   - Speaking is a physically stressful experience that can cause a rise in blood pressure, irregular heartbeat and, in extreme cases, profuse sweating.
   - Physical tension increases nervousness and can have an adverse effect on the parts of the body that produce voice.
   - Breathing is the foundation of good delivery.
   - Use simple relaxation and breathing exercises to combat the causes of tension.
   - Don't worry if some nervousness remains – your aim should be to minimise it rather than completely eliminate it.
   - Alcohol is never the answer.

Conclusion

Speaking with Confidence

We take it for granted that good sporting performances depend on the players understanding what they are doing and being equipped with the necessary technical skills. Effective public speaking is no different. But the rise of the slide-driven presentation – and some of the modern myths about the overwhelming importance of body language – makes it all too easy to think that all you need do is make sure you have plenty of slides, and not to worry too much about the words you actually use in getting your messages across. This does not work, but the methods in this book do, as they are based on the 'timeless toolkit' of great speakers past and present, whose effectiveness relied on the same easy-to-learn techniques.

This book fills the gap in the information available to speakers, and equips them with the techniques to produce an effective performance. However, as with music and sport, knowing what to do and how to do it are not enough on their own to guarantee success. Like any other activity involving knowledge and technique, effectiveness depends on practice – and the more you practise, the better you get.

The trouble is that slide-dependent presenting – the current industry-standard model – is so firmly entrenched in the culture of companies and organisations that people often see it as too radical a step to start doing things differently. However, as was mentioned in Step 3, those who are 'daring' enough to abandon slides in favour of boards and flip charts typically achieve better rapport with their audiences than they have ever experienced before.

Shortly after attending one of my courses, a woman who had been summoned to give a presentation to the main board of her company decided to take what she saw as a major risk. She prepared a script along the lines described in Step 2, used a lot of the techniques from Step 4 and rehearsed it several times beforehand. At the end of the presentation, the chairman rose to his feet – not as she initially feared to dismiss or demote her but to congratulate her on what he described as 'the best presentation anyone has ever given in this boardroom'. Her reputation as a good communicator began to spread, and she found herself being asked to give more presentations on behalf of the company. This has not only given her more opportunities to practise, but has also significantly improved her confidence and career prospects.

This example is evidence of a deep groundswell of dissatisfaction with the industry-standard model of presentation, and a greater receptiveness to change than is commonly thought to be the case by those who worry about doing things differently. If this is so, then the climate is right to replace the current orthodoxy with a renewed confidence in the power of the spoken word. But this depends on many more people taking action than a few converts who happen to have attended a course. So another reason for writing this book is to put the case for change to a wider audience of readers. My hope is that you will not only benefit personally from using this tried-and-tested approach to public speaking, but will also become an active campaigner for change.

When it comes to speaking effectively in public, the only thing that separates the hesitant majority from the gifted few is an understanding of the needs of audiences and the techniques that meet those needs. Where the gifted minority have the edge is in having had the good luck to be blessed with an intuitive grasp of how to do it. The rest of us need to work at it, but the good news is that everyone who is able to get messages across in a private conversation is capable of doing the same in public. Time and again, I have seen people who used to dread public speaking discover that they get a real buzz from achieving a good rapport with an audience. The great thing is that anyone can do it, once they know how. And if you follow the steps in this book, you'll be able to do it too.

Useful Resources for Speech-makers

Great Speeches

For getting a feel for the language and structures of effective speech-making, you can't beat reading (and preferably reading aloud), listening to or watching famous speeches of the past and present. These are widely available in books, CDs, DVDs and on the internet. Some websites enable you to download both recordings and the full scripts of speeches, which makes it easy to learn about how great speakers go about delivering speeches (pausing, stressing certain words, etc.) from a written text.

Dictionaries of Quotations

These are widely available in bookshops and on various internet sites, and, as was seen in Step 4, an apt quotation can be an effective way of introducing or illustrating a point – providing, of course, it is relevant to your subject matter.

Dictionaries of Dates

Sometimes, you can increase interest and impact by pointing out that some famous (or infamous) event took place on the anniversary of the day on which you are making a speech or presentation. Dictionaries of dates provide an easy and instant way of checking whether there is any scope for doing this.

Dictionaries of Synonyms and Antonyms

Given the importance of contrasts, as discussed in Step 4, the ease of access to antonyms (i.e. words with directly opposite meanings) in dictionaries of synonyms and antonyms is another useful aid to creativity, and included in the 'thesaurus' function of most leading word-processing programs.

Word-Game Dictionaries

Books are available listing words that are acceptable within the rules of various word-games, such as *Scrabble*. If you are looking to create a sequence involving alliteration (see Step 4 on the 'sound of words') and are looking for a word that begins with the same letter as some other word,

word-game dictionaries have an advantage over conventional dictionaries, because the absence of several lines of definitions means that you can scan through a list of words much more quickly and easily.

Index